The Roads of the Roma

– a PEN anthology of Gypsy writers –

edited by

Ian Hancock

Siobhan Dowd

Rajko Djurić

Published by University of Hertfordshire Press

On behalf of PEN American Center

The Roads of the Roma is a publication
in the *Threatened Literatures* series
of the Freedom-to-Write Committee
of PEN American Center.

Its publication would not have been possible
without the support of The Open Society Institute.

.

PEN American Center is the American branch of PEN,
the worldwide writers association that
promotes the cause of literatures everywhere and
defends the freedom of the written word.

The Freedom-to-Write Committee aids writers who face repression
and censorship around the globe and, through its *Threatened
Literatures* series, supports languages and literatures emanating
from communities of writers under attack as a result of an
intolerant government or social climate.

First published 1998
Reprinted April 2004
University of Hertfordshire Press
University of Hertfordshire
College Lane
Hatfield
Hertfordshire AL10 9AD

©PEN American Center

ISBN 0 900458 90 9

Designed by
Lisa Cordes

Cover design
based on a photograph by
David Gallant

Printed by
Antony Rowe Ltd

Acknowledgements

The Editors of *The Roads of the Roma* wish to thank the following people without whom this book would never have become a reality:

First and foremost the contemporary Gypsy writers from twenty countries whose poems and prose extracts are contained in this anthology;

Aryeh Neier of The Open Society Institute for his warm support;

Donald Kenrick for giving us most of the information and entries in the chronology and acting as an invaluable consultant generally;

Alexian Santino Spinelli for sending us his collections of Romani poems and for helping us with numerous queries;

Bill Forster and Lisa Cordes of the University of Hertfordshire Press – their words of encouragement and thoughtful input have been invaluable;

Marcel Cortiade who generously shared with us much of his own carefully collected Romani works;

Sinéad ní Shuinéar who advised us on the work of the Irish Traveller Chrissie Ward;

All the members of the Romani PEN Club who collaborated with us;

All the translators who undertook this work with enthusiasm and care, for very little recompense;

The widely scattered members of the Romnet mailing list on the Internet who helped fill the gaps in the biographies of the contributors;

And to Diana Ayton-Shenker, Karen Kennerly, Isabelle Stockton and Sara Whyatt and everyone at PEN in New York and London who gave a helping hand to this project;

And finally, the editors join with PEN American Center in extending their special thanks to The Open Society Institute for funding this project and for its support of PEN's freedom-to-write work generally.

In memory of
Leksa Manuš
1942 – 1997

We were silent for thousands of years,
but our hearts are full
of unuttered sentences,
like a sea receiving
blue river waters
all its life long.

– from *The People With the Face of the Sun* by Dezider Banga –

CONTENTS

Introduction

Ian Hancock

The heart, the soul and the history of the Romani people – of whom I am one – are embodied in the Romani language. In this volume, the writings of thirty authors have been brought together in a PEN anthology of the literature of the Roma, as one in its *Threatened Literatures* series. Over half was originally written in Romani, with versions by their authors in different European languages, including Polish, Italian, French and German. And while those presented here are for the most part in English translation, their spirit has nevertheless been successfully maintained by Burton Bollag, Siobhan Dowd, Tom Fugalli, Ian MacAndless, Minna Proctor, Sinéad ní Shuinéar and Anika Weiss and others who have done a remarkable job of capturing the feel, the heart, and the soul of the originals.

But in this introduction I shall deal mostly with history, for its presence in poetry is sometimes obscure, and furthermore it has been recast and reinterpreted to such a degree, that most of the information which is readily available succeeds only in adding to the mystification which seems always to have accompanied writings on Roma.

While hundreds of poems, plays, operas and novels have been written with Roma characters or themes, virtually none of them have been written by Roma themselves, and fewer still by writers with any real acquaintance with the Romani people. This has resulted in the emergence, over the years, of a literary, fictitious "Gypsy" image, and an equally unreal history. For some authors our people came from the Moon, while for others we originated in Atlantis or, as Marilyn Brown discusses (1985:22), in a race of "prehistoric troglodytes". Even the most recent encyclopedia and dictionary entries qualify their academic accounts of Romani history with words and phrases such as "mysterious", "thought by some", "supposedly" (from India) and so on. Even as this introduction was being written, a fax came into the Romani Union office which was an announcement notifying us of a lavish programme of Roma music and dance taking place in New York, with visiting ensembles from various European countries, and which explained that "the Gypsies... constitute a people with no written history, whose roots are shrouded in mystery and yet whose culture has had a profound effect throughout the world".

It is hardly to be wondered then, that the perception of Gypsies remains nebulous, and Gypsies themselves remain a mystified population, "full of riddles and confusions, and surrounded by an aura of secrecy", as one author sees it (Shcherbakova, 1984:1).

A double standard clearly operates: for example it is a fact that the vast majority of human populations lack their own written history, and so Roma are not noteworthy in this respect − but attention is drawn to it nevertheless in the account which reached us by fax. Because of this persistent desire to mystify and otherize, an unreal history has emerged constructed by outsiders, and which is perpetuated from generation to generation in both fictional and non-fictional literature. Brown *(loc. cit.)* has elaborated on this:

> "Although the Indian origin of the Gypsies has been proved linguistically by the fact that Romani, their language, was derived from Sanskrit, most nineteenth-century writers preferred to promote an enigma. Even today, Gypsies remain an anomaly to the degree that their migrations, which began about AD 1000, escape the usual religious, biologic, geographic, economic and political structures used to explain migration as a sociological phenomenon. But the nineteenth century actively cultivated popular legends and theories that obfuscated what little 'scientific' explanations existed. These legends . . . represented an effort by civilized Europeans to justify the sense of primitivism inspired in them by Gypsies, [who] were the lost link with the ancient and hermetic wisdom of the East. The primitive and inexplicable natural force that determined their wandering instinct was thought to be superior to and stronger than modern industrial progress."

Part of the conventional description insists, as it did in the illustration given here, that we are a "people without letters", and sometimes that even our *oral* narrative has really been appropriated from the non-Romani populations around us. If we are indeed a people without any kind of literary heritage, then we are obliged to wonder why, in the few years since the opening up of eastern Europe, Gypsy literature has flourished in such overwhelming abundance, making at first sight anomalous the inclusion of such an anthology in the PEN "Threatened Literatures" series. But this cornucopia of poetry and prose did not spring into existence overnight and unnourished; it came from somewhere, and its origins run deep and old in the Romani experience and lie in a long era of being silenced.

We were silent for thousands of years
But our hearts are full
of unuttered sentences,
like a sea receiving
blue river waters
all its life long

From *The People With the Face of the Sun*
by Dezider Banga

Though we no longer question the validity of the oxymoronic term 'oral literature' the question of what Romani literature is, whether oral or written, should be addressed here, for if it includes the plethora of material with Gypsy characters' or Gypsy themes, then most of its writers aren't Roma at all. Likewise we must ask whether it is still Romani literature when the author is Romani but the topic is not – like numbers of the entries in the *Great Romani Encyclopedia* now in process of compilation. For the purposes of this anthology, Romani literature means that both the writer and the topic are Romani even if, in the latter instance, the associations are sometimes opaque.

The growth of written literature has been matched by the paintings and drawings of Koći, Károly, Dzúrko, Stojka and others; and while most of the contributions to this volume consist of poetry, another genre of written literature has been that of journals and magazines, some of which date back to the first decades of this century, and most of which have served as vehicles for original essays and poems. The earliest published effort probably appeared in Russia in 1915, when Aleksander Germano produced a small essay in the Romani language in the town of Orlo. Germano also translated existing works into Romani, including those by Pushkin and Gorki. In addition he wrote a grammar of Romani, a history of the Roma, and helped establish the Teatr Romen.

It is evident from the selections here that certain themes recur in Romani narrative, which may even be arranged in a kind of logical sequence. Thus there are the poems by Manuš, Maya, Spinelli and others which reach to our distant Indian roots, and there are those by e.g. Lolyeshti celebrating Romani identity; Banga and Manuš write of migration and a closeness with nature.

Perhaps many also lament a loss of freedom: the poems of Hedges, Reiznerová and Spinelli long for earlier days, no doubt made happier in retrospect by the passing of time. The ubiquitous references to flowers and the wind and the rain in Romani poetry seem to have become a surrogate outdoors for sedentary Romani writers in the late twentieth century.

Regret for having been born in the non-Romani world underlies Jimmy Story's defence of the "new Rom" – Roma who have had to learn about the Romani language and experience from books, and who have perhaps only learnt of their Romani ancestry in later life. Leksa Manuš on the other hand sympathises with the position of the emerging Romani intelligentsia who, despite their existence in and responsibility to two worlds, have still to learn from all Roma and must never abandon their roots. Manuš also repeats the belief he maintained fiercely while he was alive, that "strength is in literacy." Intellectual conflict with the non-Gypsy world is also the theme in poems by Smith and Kwiek, who berate the non-Roma "Gypsy experts" for defining Roma and Romani existence. The greatest number of poems, however, including most of those which were not selected for this anthology, address daily encounters with prejudice and persecution. Along with the blossoming of Romani literature in the post-Communist period, has emerged hand-in-glove a frightening increase in racist violence against Romani populations in Europe; the latest entries from Donald Kenrick's chronology serialized in the pages of this volume reflect this trend in an alarming way, telling of skinhead, neo-nazi and neo-fascist assaults upon Roma chillingly characterized by brutalization and murder. The reasons for this are complex, but at their root remain incomprehensible, for here is a population with no aspirations to territory or to political domination, a population which has started no war, and which wants nothing more than to be left in peace and to enjoy civil and legal equality.

Antigypsyism is nothing new. In a letter to George Sand a hundred and thirty years ago, which might have been written today (reproduced in Conard, 1929:309), Gustav Flaubert commented on this and offered an explanation for it:

> "[I visited] a camp of Gypsies at Rouen... they excite the *hatred* of the bourgeois even though inoffensive as sheep... that hatred is linked to something deep and complex; it is found in all orderly people. It is the hatred that they feel for the bedouin, the heretic, the philosopher, the solitary, the poet and there is fear in that hatred."

Still other contributions to this collection deal with the *Porrajmos* – the Romani Holocaust – specifically. The intensely moving prose narrative by Rajko Djurić is just one example. Self-denigration, perhaps a psychological by-product of constant oppression, is a theme in the writings of Hancock, Kwiek and Maya, who asks "is there something wrong with me, because I'm a Gypsy?". A passage from Maximoff's *The Price of Freedom* is included here because it provides a cameo from the period of Gypsy slavery in Romania, a crucial time in Romani history.

Gregory Kwiek's poem alludes to the angry reaction many Roma express when first learning about this oppressive period, which lasted for more than five centuries.

In the United States, where most of the Roma are descendants of the slaves liberated from the Wallachian estates 140 years ago, this memory has been obliterated; in American Vlax Romani, the word for "slave", *rrobo*, now means only "one unwilling to work."

It is perhaps odd that Romani history is a closed book for Roma – and it isn't that the word "book" is an operative one here, for certainly there are traditionally non-literate peoples who know their own history. It has been suggested that centuries of oppression, documented in the chronology throughout this book, have obliterated any desire to look back. Nostalgia, they say, is for those with happier histories. Roma who know any history at all have acquired it from books written by *gadjé* (non-Roma) or else from folk memory; the notion of an origin in Egypt, once widespread in Europe, is still found amongst Roma. The story of being obliged to keep on the move because of having forged Christ's nails, obviously a myth of non-Gypsy origin, is everywhere repeated in Romani populations. While an American Rom can tell you that his family came from Russia or Serbia, that is usually where the history stops, and that is why a discussion of history finds a place here. One writer goes so far as to consider this characteristic an integral part of being Rom: "Ancient history", she's on record as saying, "for most [Roma], consisted of the earliest memory of the oldest living person among them. And this not – knowing distinguished them, even if they were hardly conscious of it. It was, I came to believe, a defining attribute of Gypsy identity" (Fonseca, 1995).

So what do we know? What *is* the current state of our knowledge of Romani history? There have been many accounts of it, mostly fanciful, less often approaching plausibility, but it has only been in the past very few years that a likely explanation has begun to emerge.

We know that the Roma have been made up of many different groups of people from the very beginning, and have absorbed outsiders throughout their history. Because they arrived in Europe from the East, they were thought by the first Europeans to be from Turkey or Nubia or Egypt, or any number of vaguely acknowledged non-European places, and they were called, among other things, *Egyptians* or *'Gyptians*, which is where the word "Gypsy" comes from. In some places, this Egyptian identity was taken entirely seriously, and was no doubt borrowed by the early Roma themselves. In the fifteenth-century James V of Scotland concluded a treaty with a local Romani leader pledging the support of his armies to help recover "Little Egypt" (an old name for Epirus, on the Greek-Albanian coast) for them. Another façade adopted by the first Roma in Europe was that of religious penitents, which allowed them to carry documents ostensibly signed by the Pope and by King Ladislaus requesting their protection. But this was not a uniquely Romani ploy, and was probably inspired by various European migrant populations such as the Rubins, the Coquillarts, the Convertis or the Golliards in France, who were doing the same thing.

It was not until the second half of the eighteenth-century that scholars in Europe began to realise that the Romani language in fact came from India. Basic words, such as some numerals and kinship terms, and names for body parts, actions and so on, were demonstrably Indian. So – they concluded – if the language were originally Indian, its speakers very likely must be as well.

Once they realised this, their next questions were the obvious ones: if Roma were indeed from India, when did they leave, and why, and are there *still* Roma in that country?

An answer seemed to be ready-made in a book called the *Shah Nameh* (the *Book of Kings*), an historical account of the life and times of Bahram Gur, a fifth-century Persian shah. It contained an account of a gift which was made by the Maharaja of Sindh, in India, to Bahram Gur's court, of ten thousand musicians. After a year, the story continued, the musicians had all disappeared.

Nineteenth-century scholars thought that this explanation answered many of their questions, especially because there is still today a population of Indian origin living in the Middle East called the Doms, and who speak a language also readily traceable to India. The Roma in Europe, they reasoned, were part of that same early population who kept on moving westwards leaving the Doms behind in Asia, and so the *Shah Nameh* account continues to be repeated, uncritically, in even the most recent books about Roma.

Although this story is still finding favour with journalists and others, few academics at the end of the twentieth-century believe it any more, because we have a much greater understanding now of Indian languages and history. Romani and the language of the Doms (*Domari*), while both ultimately Indian, are very different from each other; their shared vocabulary is less than ten per cent and even demonstrably cognate Indian forms are fewer than two thirds. The similarities which do exist are because they are both Indian – just as they exist between Romani and Gujerati, say, or Romani and Bengali – and not because they were once the same language. There are also linguistic features in Romani which tell us that its original speakers must have left India in the eleventh-century or later, and not six hundred years earlier in the fifth-century. And when we also examine the words which Romani adopted from other languages along the migratory route, we can get an idea of who the early Roma came into contact with, which in turn tells us *where* that must have happened. An example can be taken from one language called *Burushaski*. There are a handful of words from this language, such as those for 'pull' and 'how many', but it is only spoken in a tiny area high in the mountain passes out of northern India, in the Hindu Kush. Another language spoken near here is *Phalura*, which has also provided Romani with a number of words, such as 'son-in-law', 'walnut' and 'sleep'. The fact that they are *only* spoken in such small and specific areas and nowhere else, and keeping in mind what the linguistic picture must have been like a millennium ago, we have to accept that this was the place through which the first Roma left India.

Clues like this help to answer when and where, but not who or why. However, if we look at the vocabulary of Romani, we find indications of a specifically military history. For example, the most common word for someone who is not a Rom is *gadjo*, and this comes from an old Indian word *gajjha*, meaning 'civilian' or 'non-military person'. Another word for a non-Rom is *das*, which originally meant a prisoner of war, and which means 'slave' in modern Hindi and Panjabi. Yet another is *gomi*, from a word for 'one who has surrendered', presumably as a captive taken in war. It has the same form and meaning in Bangani, a modern Indian language. A fourth word for a non-Romani person is *goro*, which in some Indian languages such as Hindi, means 'pale-skinned person'. but which in others, e.g. Sindhi, means 'captive' or 'slave'. The words for 'sword', 'battlecry', 'spear' and 'gaiters' are also all Indian, and all belong to the military semantic domain. A further possible connection with the Rajputs is the fact that their ancient clan emblems, symbols of the sun and the moon, survive among some Roma in Europe today with a similar function (Sutherland, 1975:125). With these kinds of clues, the next step was to discover what soldiers, if any, were in the Hindu Kush in the eleventh-century.

At the very beginning of that century, India came under attack by the Muslim general Mahmud of Ghazni, who was trying to push Islam eastwards into India, which was mainly Hindu territory. The Indian rulers had been assembling troops to hold back the Muslim army for several centuries already, deliberately drawing their warriors from various populations who were not Aryan. The Aryans had moved into India many centuries before, and had pushed the original population down into the south, or else had absorbed them into the lowest strata of their own society which began to separate into different social levels or castes, called *varnas* (colours) in Sanskrit, each one higher than the other, with the Brahmins or holy men at the very top, then the Kshatriyas or warriors below them, the Vaisnas or merchants and producers below them, and the non-Aryan Shudras at the bottom. It was forbidden to marry, or even touch, a person who was not from the same caste as oneself.

The Aryans regarded Aryan life as being more precious than non-Aryan life, and would not risk losing it in battle. So the troops which were assembled to fight the armies of Mahmud of Ghazni were all drawn from non-Aryan populations, and made honorary members of the Kshattriya or Warrior caste and allowed to wear their battledress and insignia.

They were taken from many different ethnic groups who spoke a wide variety of languages and dialects. Some were Lohars and Gujjars, some were Tandas, some were Rajputs, who descended from non-Indian peoples who had come to live in India some centuries before, and some may also have been Siddhis, Africans from the East African coast who fought as mercenaries for both the Hindus and the Muslims. Together they made up the Kshattriya warriors who moved within the far northern parts of India between the years AD 1001 and AD 1027 to try to prevent Ghazni's Islamic troops from entering their land. But their resistance was ultimately not successful, and northern India was eventually occupied by the Muslims, and Islam remains the major religion throughout the area today.

This composite army moved out of India through the mountain passes and west into Persia, battling with Muslim forces all along the eastern limit of Islam. While this is to an extent speculative, it is based upon sound linguistic and historical evidence, and provides the best-supported scenario to date. We can even more cautiously venture to establish a particular year for the exodus out of India. Of the seventeen Ghaznavid raids between AD 1001 and AD 1027, only two of them took place in the area which matches the linguistic evidence, and the second of these was the Muslims' greatest defeat. These took place in Kashmir, in 1013 and 1015, and the Ghaznavids were chased westwards out of the Hindu Kush.

Those involved in unravelling Romani history are not only examining the linguistic and historical material they *do* have, but are also looking at earlier hypotheses in an attempt to validate or dismiss them by process of elimination. Thus we cannot place the migration of the ancestors of the Roma out of India before the eleventh- century, because of certain linguistic characteristics which didn't exist at an earlier time. If we are reluctant to accept those things which point to a military history – the original meanings of the various words for non-Gypsy, for instance, or the apparent retention of Rajput clan insignia amongst some Vlax populations in Europe today, we are left having to accept that these parallels are merely coincidence, and having to provide alternative explanations. And while it has been suggested by some scholars that the Romani migration consisted of many different groups leaving India at different times over a period of centuries, we are left having to explain how such groups, separated by vast distances of time and space, managed to relocate and reunite into the one population which eventually entered Europe. We can also venture to specify the route taken out of India, not only because of the non-Indic lexical adoptions which are found in Romani, but because of what we *don't* find: significant representations from Semitic or Turkic languages, for instance. And since there were only a few roads through the mountains out of India, the geographical possibilities are narrowed down even further.

Because Islam was not only making inroads into India to the east, but was also being spread westwards into Europe, this conflict carried the Indian troops – the early Roma – further and further in that direction, until they eventually crossed over into south-eastern Europe about the year 1300.

Not all of the Kshattriya warriors left India. Some of those who remained continue to be known as *Rajputs*, which means 'sons of kings', and while they see themselves today as true descendants of the Kshattriya caste, the Brahmins delight in reminding them that they were drawn from the Shudras. Some populations in India which identify themselves as Rajputs, such as the Banjara, also recognize that they are related to the Roma outside of India, and make an effort to keep in contact with Romani organizations in Europe and America.

One problem has been that when the British were occupying India, they applied the label *gypsies* in a broad way to numbers of nomadic groups in that country who had nothing at all to do with real "Gypsies", i.e. Roma. Only some of those populations are connected with the history described here, and with the Roma throughout the world. But it has had the misleading effect that Westerners have assumed a relationship which isn't there, and have even written books or produced documentary films perpetuating the idea of such a connection.

From the very beginning, then, the Romani population has been made up of various different peoples who have come together over time. As the ethnically and linguistically mixed occupational population from India moved further and further away from its land of origin beginning in the eleventh-century, so it began to acquire its own ethnic identity, and it was at this time that the Romani language also began to take shape. But the mixture of peoples and languages didn't stop there, for as the warriors moved northwestwards through Persia, it took words and grammar from Persian, and no doubt absorbed new members too; and the same thing happened in Armenia and in the Byzantine Empire, and has continued to happen in Europe. In some instances, the mingling of small groups of Roma with other peoples has resulted in such groups being absorbed into them and losing their Romani identity; the Jenische are perhaps such an example. In others, it has been the outsiders who have been absorbed, and who, in the course of time, have become one with the Romani group.

In Europe, the Roma were either kept in slavery in the Balkans (in territory which is today Romania), or else were able to move on and up into the rest of the continent, reaching every northern and western country by about 1500. In the course of time, as a result of having interacted with various European populations and being fragmented into widely-separated groups, the Roma have emerged today as a continuum of distinct ethnic groups constituting a larger whole. While non-Roma specialists tend to classify these divisions according to linguistic criteria, the same distinctions perceived within the Romani population are far more complex, incorporating national and occupational as well as dialectal boundaries. Some groups reject the term Rom, others regard the label as their exclusive property. It has been divisions such as these which have led some writers, both academic and political, to deny that Roma constitute a single people at all. In its extreme form, this position holds that Roma are a population of eclectic, local, non-Asian origin artificially constructed by the writers of European literature (see for example Sandland, 1996, Wexler, 1996, and Willems, 1997). Certainly such divisions can be exaggerated and manipulated if the differences separating various populations are emphasized, and the inherited linguistic and cultural factors which all Romani groups have in common to a greater or lesser degree, are minimized.

Everything that separates Romani populations from each other has been acquired from outside, while everything that links them shares a common origin outside of Europe. When Roma meet, it is our common heritage that binds us and that we seek out, not the variously acquired, non-Romani aspects of our culture and speech. It is our speech which is the greatest part of that heritage, and even among those populations whose Romani has been reduced to only a vocabulary, as in England or Spain or Scandinavia, it remains a powerful ingredient in Romani ethnic identity.

Today, the Romani language, like the Romani people and Romani culture, remains at heart Indian, despite being modified through contact with others over the years. Those who have maintained that Romani is somehow less than legitimate as a language, or that its Indianness survives only in fragments (see most recently, for example, Horvath & Wexler, 1997), should do well to remember that it has retained more Indian lexical roots and grammatical morphology than there are Anglo-Saxon roots and morphology identifiable in modern English.

Just as Roma have been misrepresented as a people, so the Romani language has had to stand aloof from those who have claimed that it is not a real or a complete language. Its ownership has been co-opted by writer after writer, who have seen fit to create and pass off spurious Romani words to their colleagues in displays of academic dishonesty which would not be tolerated for a moment in other linguistic disciplines (Grant, 1995).

Dishonesty is also a characteristic fundamental to the Roma stereotype; Isabel Fonseca (*op. cit., p.15*) cautioned her readers that: "Gypsies lie. They lie a lot – more often and more inventively than other people". This assumption, of course, simply reflects the imbalance of control over Romani identity, since statements originating from Roma which are not what the investigator wants to hear, can simply be dismissed as "lies".

Elsewhere I have shown that the foolish and offensive idea that the Romani people are devoid of the concepts of *ownership, obligation, beauty, truth*, etc., has been fostered by writers whose "evidence" for this is supported by their confident, though naive, assertions that words for these things are lacking in the Romani language (Hancock, 1998). The same essay addresses the equally silly claim that we as a people think only in the present, and as a result have no means of constructing the future tense in our language. Along with statements such as "Gypsies don't feel pain like other people," or "Gypsies actually enjoyed the punishments meted out to them during slavery" (both found in Hancock, 1987), or that we are dirty because of an "innate fear of water", or that we *prefer* to live next to garbage dumps, given a choice (the basis for at least three cartoons in the Romani Union Archives) when it is usually the only place the local borough council will provide. Such observations succeed only in reinforcing a 'gypsy' image which is diametrically opposed to the Romani reality. Since Roma have traditionally lacked a voice in the mainstream domain, such statements have been allowed to pass unchallenged.

Cause for concern too is the fact that this anti-Roma bias is especially evident in children's literature, and is therefore aimed specifically at a population whose social attitudes, which will carry them through the rest of their lives, are in the process of being formed. The very fact of being a Rom was likened to a disease, for example, in the August 1996 issue of *Disney Adventures: The Magazine for Kids*. Here, in an issue devoted to the then recently-released cartoon *Hunchback of Notre Dame*, its young readers were advised to beware of a condition called "gypsyitis," the symptoms of which included "an urge to run away from it all and dance among the dandelions", and to being "footloose and fancy-free" instead of a "buckle-down, rules-and-regulations kinda person." Editor Phyllis

Erlich defended the magazine's position in a response to a letter of protest from the Romani Union, saying that it was, after all, "a positive portrayal of the Gypsy spirit." As long as what constitutes our spirit – and consequently *us* – is defined by those who operate the non-Roma media, we will be denied control of our identity in the same arena. And as long as we as 'gypsies' continue to be regarded in a trivial and light-hearted manner, we can never hope to have our real, day-to-day problems taken seriously.

While we suffer physically on the streets of Europe, we are targeted in a different but just as significant way in literature. Both situations are equally oppressive, and both are provoking differing responses from the Romani people. In Slovakia and the Czech Republic, some Roma activists have, as a last resort, urged the Romani populations to arm themselves with sticks and guns. In Romania, in an effort to safeguard their homes and families, organised groups of Roma youth have formed to protect themselves against bands of white villagers. This is resistance on the physical front. On the literary front, *achel o por maj zoralo e xanrrestar*, the pen remains always mightier than the sword, and it is through the written word, and collections such as this, that the battle is also being fought. PEN deserves our warmest gratitude for making this publication, and the *PEN Romani Voice* (Djurić and Gilsenbach) possible. In the electronic world too, the World Wide Web supports numbers of Roma sites which broadcast and exchange information. And for the past five years, Romnet, an internet list-server, has united Roma and non-Roma sympathizers on every continent, and has stimulated successful letter-writing campaigns and protests. Gypsynet, restricted to Roma-only subscribers, does the same thing. Roma-run websites such as *Patrin* and *Rroma Yekhipe* reproduce current articles on Roma from the world press, and make such resources available to everyone.

This book brings to the English-speaking world for the very first time writings not just *about* Roma but *by* Roma, and will, one foresees, play an important role in laying to rest the stereotypes which stand between the Romani peoples and their acceptance as real and feeling members of the human community.

References

Acton, Thomas, & Gary Mundy, eds., 1997. *Romani culture and Gypsy identity*. Hatfield: University of Hertfordshire Press.

Brown, Marilyn, 1985. *Gypsies and Other Bohemians: The Myth of the Artist in Nineteenth-Century France*. Ann Arbor: UMI Research Press.

Conard, V., 1929. *Gustave Flaubert: Correspondance*. Paris.

Djurić, Rajko, & Reimar Gilsenbach, eds., 1996-. *Stimme des Romani PEN: Die Zeitschrift der Roma-Schriftsteller aller Länder*. Berlin: Romani PEN Zentrums.

Fonseca, Isabel, 1995. *Bury Me Standing: The Gypsies and their Journey*. New York: Random House.

Grant, Anthony, 1995. "Plagiarism and lexical orphans in the European Romani lexicon", in Matras, ed., 1995:53-68.

Hancock, Ian, 1987. *The Pariah Syndrome: An Account of Gypsy Slavery and Persecution*. Ann Arbor: Karoma Publishers.

Hancock, Ian, 1998. "Duty and beauty, possession and truth: the claim of lexical impoverishment as control," in Acton and Mundy, 1997.

Horvath, Julia, & Paul Wexler (eds.), 1997. *Relexification in Creole and non-Creole languages, with special Attention to Haitian Creole, Modern Hebrew, Romani and Romanian*. Wiesbaden: Harrassowitz.

Matras, Yaron, ed., 1995. *Romani in Contact*. Amsterdam & Philadelphia: John Benjamins.

Sandland, Ralph, 1996. "The real, the simulacrum and the construction of 'gypsy' in law", *Journal of Law and Society*, 23(3):383-405.

Shcherbakova, V., 1984. *Gypsy Musical Performance in Russia*. Moscow: Academia Nauk.

Sutherland, Anne, 1975. *Gypsies, the Hidden Americans*. London: Macmillan.

Wexler, Paul, 1996. "Could there be a Rotwelsch origin for the Romani lexicon?", Paper presented at the Third International conference on Romani Linguistics, Prague.

Willems, Wim, 1998. *In Search of the True Gypsy*. New York: Cass.

Editors' note

This anthology has been structured around the history of the Romani people, as this is, we believe, indivisible from their literature. Readers will find the poems woven into the chronology as and when a poem seemed to tie in with a particular entry or group of entries.

There were many writings to choose from and our task was not an easy one, but a desire to speak to our theme of the Roma's history of repression and injustice – even where this was elliptical rather than directly stated – guided most of our selections. However, there are some exceptions. In some – *Ars Poetica* by Loleshtye, *Son of the wind* by Alexian Santino Spinelli, *Give me a string to play on* by Djura Makhotin – there is more of a tone of celebration; and Jose Heredia Maya's *Eleven laments* would seem more of a poem about intimate love in its intention, but was included for the haunting quality of its underlying sombreness.

It was throughout our intention to present the literature of the present, but in two cases we broke this rule and included works by two authors who have died. First, Papusza, the renowned Romani poet from Poland whom many regard as the mother of Romani literature, and second, Leksa Manuš, to whom this book is dedicated. He died in 1997 but is remembered fondly by the Romani generation coming after him both for his stature as a poet and for the generous encouragement he gave to younger writers.

Also, the works are all by Romani people themselves, again with two exceptions. We decided to include the fragmented and beautiful poem by Mariella Mehr who is a Jenische writer from Switzerland – the Jenische are not usually regarded, strictly speaking, as Romani, although there may be some historical connection between the two peoples. However, the Jenische's history of their children being taken from their families and put into care – a fate which befell Mariella Mehr herself – is one shared by travelling people of all kinds. The same thinking applied to the Irish Traveller Chrissie Ward. Irish Travellers are most certainly not related to the Roma, but Ward's description of the authorities' attempts to thwart the Travellers' camp sites speaks to the general difficulties in this regard. Oral literature was also not included, but we made another exception, and on similar grounds, of Ward's orally-given memories of her father, who died in mysterious circumstances in police custody.

Readers will find that we switch between the words "Gypsy" and "Rom" (usually singular but sometimes used to refer to the people as a collective noun) and "Gypsies" and "Roma." These editors definitely prefer the words "Rom" and Roma" – which are also spelt sometimes with a double r. However, "Gypsy" is so commonly used by both Roma and non-Roma (or "gadjé") that it is hard to avoid, but it is, in its origin, a misnomer, as it is now known that the Roma did not come from "Egypt". "Romani" is the general adjective, but is also used to refer to the language the Roma speak as well.

Finally, a note on the translations. Many of these poems were originally written in one of the Romani dialects, others in standard Romani, and others again in one of the author's other main languages. Because of the fact that there are very few people qualified to translate literary works from Romani directly into English, we have sometimes had to rely on our translators working with intermediate versions in such languages as French or Italian. Wherever possible, we have checked the resulting translation against the original.

In some cases, readers will find that no translator has been credited. This is invariably because the translator did not identify himself or herself in the edition we were using and we were unable to find out who had done the translation. The translations in question were often literal, in faulty English, and the editors have done their best to present them in corrected English in a way that does as much justice to the original as possible. We apologise for any misrepresentations that might have crept in, although in most cases we have been able to check our work with the authors themselves and they have granted us both their permission to use the work and their approval of the translation we are using.

In each case, every possible effort has been made to obtain copyright permission from the authors. The editors apologise to any authors we have been unsuccessful in locating by time of press.

Biographies of all the editors, authors, and translators are at the back of the book.

The Roads of the Roma

Leksa Manuš (Latvia)

Each night, my God, as I close my eyes,
I see before me the roads of the Roma.
But where, my God, is the long-lost road,
the one true road, the one first-travelled?

The countries of Europe are riddled
with roads: across Russia and Poland,
Lithuania and Latvia they weave,
they criss-cross Scandinavia.

These are the roads I roam each night,
in search of the one true road,
the road the travellers first travelled,
the road of my Romani forebears.

Through Germany and the Balkan hills
of Hungary and Romania I wander,
reaching the land of that ancient empire,
Byzantium. In centuries gone by,

the Roma migrated here, lived cheek by cheek
with Greeks, Jews, Slavs, and Turks.
They live here still, still poor and plotless,
Travellers from some distant land.

From Europe I follow the roads of the Roma
into the orient: to Armenia and Iran where
the Sassanids once ruled, and before them
the Achaemenids. From here the road leads

to another land where the Indus-river flows
to the land where the Kushans once held sway:
This was called Gandhara, or Roma-land, here lay
the estates of the Sindhu, where our elders walked,

performing great works in sunlit fields.

Farther my road does not go; it only
goes backward into time, diving deep into
the centuries. Here, five thousand years ago,
was a land of thriving towns, Harappa

and Mohenjo-Daro among them, a land whose peoples
lived as peers, the place where our travels
began. Everything started here. What used to be
and what will be converge at this point: at the end

of that first Romani road lies the fate of my people.

The long road
of the Roma begins...

997
Ghaznavid raids into India begin and last until AD 1026.
Some Rajputs begin to leave and move West.

c1050 Byzantium
Acrobats and animal doctors (called athingani) in
Constantinople, hence the name Tsi(n)gani, later applied
to the Roma.

1192 India
Battle of Terain. Last Roma leave India for the West.

1322 Crete
Nomads reported on the island.

1347 Byzantium
Black death reaches Constantinople. Roma move west again.

1348 Serbia
Roma in Prizren.

1362 Croatia
Roma in Dubrovnik.

1373 Corfu
Gypsies reported on the island.

1378 Bulgaria
Roma living in villages near Rila Monastery.

1384 Greece
Romani shoemakers in Modon.

1385 Romania
First recorded transaction of Gypsy slaves.

The price of liberty

by Matéo Maximoff (France)

I

The Romanian countryside was unimaginably lovely that spring. It was the middle of the nineteenth century, carriages were criss-crossing the by-ways and roads, passing by fields under the shade of avenues in bloom. A riotous chorus of migratory birds, just returned for the fine days from distant lands, accompanied them. In the distance, the mountain-tops were snow-capped, a reminder of the winter just gone.

On this spring Sunday, the people from the villages and country thereabouts were making their way to the main town. It was the first day of the annual fair, an attraction for buyers all around: wealthy merchants, the bourgeois classes, peasants, dealers, and, of course, the thieves of the neighbourhood – everyone, in short, who had business to do or goods to sell, exchange, or buy, everyone who needed something and everyone who had something to dispose of – this was the week to do it. Until the following Sunday, this town would be thronged, busier than anywhere else in the province or indeed the country. In a matter of hours, fortunes, goods and slaves would change hands and masters.

The baron Andrei, wealthiest of governors and intimate of the Prince himself, had never once missed the spring fair, not once in forty years. Tall, broad-shouldered with a beard neatly barbered to a fine point, he was a popular man, commonly said to be as just as he was generous. Despite the clement weather, he was donned in a fur and an astrakhan hat and reclined in his barouche, a blanket over his knees – a solitary figure, apart from the coachman driving.

Following him came a man of forty, riding upright on his horse with an air both rough, intelligent, and sharp of eye. This was Yon, the steward, without question the true master of Andrei's estate, with its four hundred Gypsy slaves who worked under his orders to ensure that the Baron's lands bore fruit.

After him came two wagons, of which the second was empty. In the first were a dozen Roma, there to help their master with his fresh purchases. In his fantastic wealth, he nevertheless left them on this special day in their ordinary work-garb, but though poorly dressed, they were at least clean. Only one among them seemed better-dressed, a man of thirty who acted as secretary.

Four guards on horseback brought up the rear.

The police officers moved aside in greeting to let the Baron Andrei pass – he never even threw them a glance. The town gates were thrown open and the sounds of animation grew louder. On either side of the street, the merchants arranged their wares. It was a lucky-dip: every old battered thing, threadbare clothes, utensils, trinkets without worth, but which would find a buyer.

Further on, the merchandise improved in quality. There were sumptuous fabrics, silks, flowers. Further on again, to the left, there were poultry, horses, mules, donkeys. In short, a bit of everything. And a smell hit the nostrils, a mixture of fried potatoes, sausage meat, grilled corn, and further on a whiff of fruit and then that unmistakable, delectable fragrance of sweet-cakes.

Yes, everything was for sale. Even human flesh.

II

The slave market was in full swing. The auctioneer was a Turk, a great, athletic figure with hooked mustaches and a whip in his right hand. He cast a keen and practised eye upon his potential customers. He was in his element. The crowd was restless and impatient, some shouted abuse at this colossus above them. He feigned indifference to their threats, pretending not to hear. With a mocking air, he dominated them twice over with his height on the platform and his massive width. A large smirk appeared on his face when he saw Andrei's carriage make a path through the hordes. Here was the best customer of all. He started his sales-patter:

– Gentlemen, I have the honour, one more time, for another year, and another season, to sell to you the most handsome slaves you could ever hope to find on the world market. I, Constantine, your own auctioneer, I defy you to prove me false!

He paused to allow Andrei enough time to draw nearer, so that he could get a better view of the living merchandise.

– His lordship, the mighty Baron Jeremie, died a few months back, leaving these slaves to his sons. And today, these very slaves are for sale, before your eyes, the strongest muscles in the province and if you doubt my words . . .

Some Gypsy families were pushed forwards onto the platform. To speed matters up, they were sold in lots of two, sometimes three, families. Yon the steward bought five families in two lots in the name of his master Baron Andrei. These, along with a few children, were loaded into the second cart.

In the midst of the noise, heartfelt glances were exchanged. But tears, if tears there were, fell quietly. A Gypsy, a Rom, is not ever meant to cry openly for the misfortunes of his brothers and sisters. One young Rom, by the name of Isvan, threw a rapid glance toward the second cart, to see if he knew any of these men and women who were coming to live with him.

– Thirty ducats!

The price made Isvan's head turn involuntarily. The words were pronounced in the familiar tones of Yon. Thirty ducats! Was it the Baron who was behind the bid – or Yon himself? Curiosity got the better of Isvan. He began to observe the platform carefully. There were four Roma only up there: a father, a large, muscular man of forty. Constantine proclaimed him a blacksmith. Two sons, aged 21 and 19.

– And here, the undisputed flower of Gypsy girlhood, Lena, aged 17!

– Thirty-five ducats, came a cool bid.

– Forty ducats, said Yon straight away.

Isvan noticed that the Baron himself had said nothing. Either Yon had put in his bid of his own accord, or had been given full powers to bid by old Andrei himself. In either case, it looked as if Yon was going to buy this family at any price. Why? It wasn't as if, perhaps, there was any real need for them. Certainly not, thought the young Rom, Isvan. No: he knew Yon thoroughly – this lovely girl, Lena, cowering behind her brothers on the platform, was sufficient motive for Yon to bid and buy himself these four Gypsies for forty ducats.

Translated from French by Siobhan Dowd

1399	**Bohemia** The first Gypsy is mentioned in a chronicle.
1416	**Germany** Gypsies expelled from Meissen region.
1417	**Holy Roman Empire** King Sigismund grants safe conduct to Roma at Lindau.
1418	**France** First Gypsies reported in Colmar.
	Switzerland First Roma arrive.
1419	**Belgium** First Gypsies reported in Antwerp.
1420	**Holland** First Gypsies reported in Deventer.
1422	**Italy** Gypsies come to Bologna.
1423	**Slovakia** Roma in Spissky.

Tramps

by Dezider Banga (Slovak Republic)

From where do they come,
where have they gone,
the sighs of our songs,
sighs from Romani fires,
sighs from God's heart?
The wild flowers don
ebony cloaks in the night,
their delicate cups
are filled with sighs.
Only the torrential rains
and the Lord himself knows
from how far away
they have come.

Translated from Romani by Magdalena Seleanu

1425	**Spain** Roma in Zaragoza.
1447	**Catalonia** First report of Gypsies
1453	**Constantinople** Turks capture Constantinople. Flight of some Roma westward.
1471	**Switzerland** Parliament meeting in Lucerne banishes Gypsies.
1472	**Rhine Palatinate** Duke Friedrich asks his people to help the Gypsy pilgrims.
1485	**Sicily** First reports of Gypsies.
1489	**Hungary** Roma musicians play on Czepel Island.
1492	**Spain** First draft of forthcoming law of 1499 (see below).
1493	**Italy** Gypsies expelled from Milan.
1498	**Germany (Holy Roman Empire)** Expulsion of Gypsies ordered.
1499	**Spain** Expulsion of Roma ordered by Pragmatica of the Catholic Kings.
1500	**Russia** First record of Gypsies.
1504	**France** Expulsion of the Roma ordered.

Allegory

by Sterna Weltz-Zigler (France)

Our life passed us by
like the beads on a rosary
A shoulder shrug chased away
the spaces in-between
A hole in the forehead
opened into a cave
where the tarots of memory
were jumbled pell-mell
The caravan ground into
the grooves of our pain
And a pennant flew
    misery
    dignity
    sovereignty –
Allegory
of the Rom.

Translated from French by Siobhan Dowd

The long road

Šaban Iliaz (Republic of Macedonia)

We took a road into night
unaware of where it might lead.
We left behind a great land
and started our journey of sorrow.

We strayed over many a byway
carrying our heavy loads.
We buried our dead along the way;
in the forests our fathers grew old.

In the midst of the darkest place
we sat ourselves down to rest.
We paused to revive our spirits
and as we sat there, we slept;

No bread we ate nor water drank;
not a crust passed our lips.
When morning came we got up again
and continued along the road.

1505	**Denmark** Two groups of Gypsies enter the country. **Scotland** Gypsy pilgrims arrive, probably from Spain.
1510	**Switzerland** Death penalty introduced for any Rom found in the country.
1512	**Catalonia** Roma expelled. **Sweden** First Roma arrive.
1514	**England** First mention of a Gypsy in the country.
1515	**Germany** Bavaria closes its borders to the Roma.
1516	**Portugal** The Roma are mentioned in literature.
1525	**Portugal** The Roma are banned from Portugal. **Sweden** The Roma are ordered to leave the country.
1526	**Holland** Transit of Roma across country banned.
1530	**England and Wales** Expulsion of Gypsies ordered
1534	**Slovakia** Some Roma are executed in Levoca.
1536	**Denmark** The Roma are ordered to leave the country.
1538	**Portugal** Deportation of Roma to colonies begins.
1539	**Spain** Any male found nomadising ordered by law to be sent to galleys.

If I say love I name

José Heredia Maya (Spain)

If I say love I name
the last thing I have been
on my way from lark to twilight.

Whether I hold death in my fingers
or ashes to my side
the wings of pain propel me,
blue blind, over the immense plain
of a sign, a hint; your body resembles
purple light flowing towards autumn,
naming the last thing I have been
on my way from lark to twilight.

Translated from Spanish by Ian MacAndless

Eleven laments

by José Heredia Maya (Spain)

I

Who will be there to relieve
my lonesome phantom pain
and hold me when I grieve?

II

To see if I can find
the scent that your body left
I go back and forth in the wind.

III

Anyone who comes down the street knows
there are no doors in your house
and the whole world comes and goes.

IV

If you force me to choose
between my mother and your room
you want me to lose.

V

When I envision your body
my blood rises up to you
in the corner of the sky.

VI

But I want you and you know it,
that is why you come see me
and get lost in the street.

VII

You will certainly get ahead
since everyone up to the apostle
Saint Peter has been in your bed.

VIII

I hate it like nothing else
that you changed and no longer
want me to obey myself.

IX

The worst thing is not having to die,
the worst thing is being invisible
because you close your eyes.

X

Although you know I carry a cloth
so you can bury your head.
And I know God grants an autopsy
but no burial when you're dead.

XI

There was a fallen man
alone and with nothing,
and the light of my dark eyes
was like air under his wings.

Translated from Spanish by Tom Fugalli

1540	**Scotland** Gypsies allowed to live under their own laws.
1541	**Czech lands** Roma are accused of starting a fire in Prague.
1544	**England** Gypsies deported to Norway.
1547	**Bohemia** Roma are declared outlaws and are to be expelled.
1554	**England** The death penalty is imposed for any Gypsy not leaving the country within a month.
1557	**Poland and Lithuania** Expulsion of Gypsies ordered.
1562	**England** Provision of previous Acts widened to include people who live and travel like Gypsies.
1563	**Italy** Council of Trent affirms that Gypsies cannot be priests.
1569	**Lithuania and Poland** Nomadic Gypsies to be expelled.
1573	**Scotland** Gypsies either to settle down or leave country.

Son of the wind

by Alexian Santino Spinelli (Italy)

I, son of the wind
father of the long walk ...
The vast plains of grass my back has touched,
the breath of powerful horses
and the sweet song of birds
my ears have heard.
Green trees have guided
my never-ending walk,
and waters and lands
and skies and sun
and light and heat
the days I've lived;
a tent was my home:
I felt free.
The roof protecting me now
makes me small
and these walls
so well-built
with the windows
trap me behind flowers:
a prison with bars.
The hoarse-voiced song
of a bird with no name
draws me to the window; a bird
unknown
wings disfigured
it attempts to fly,
but splashes into
empty silence,
like a drop that falls
into the river where I am floating –
I can't reach the banks
to proclaim them mine.
Water driven
by the wind of the fathers
brought my dream here –
a veil has been lowered
and I planted it here,
as if it were a flag.

Translated from Italian by Minna Proctor

Gypsy soul

by Nadia Hava-Robbins (Czechoslovakia/U.S.A)

My heart has been cut open
My blood drained in the name of freedom
What remains?
Sweet music in my veins,
Ancient dance in my broken bones.

> Happy and sad,
> My spirit sails into the unknown
> With no land, no home to call my own,
> Hopelessly searching through the past
> To find my people, who scattered
> Like glass that shattered
> Long ago.

Listen and you'll hear the song of longing
Look into the far distance beyond the horizon
And there you'll see dancing
My lonely Gypsy soul

Extracts from:

Untitled verse

by Papusza (Poland)

I love the fire as my own heart.
Winds fierce and small
rocked the Gypsy girl
and drove her far into the world.
The rains washed away her tears,
the sun – the golden Gypsy father –
warmed her tears
and wonderfully seared her heart ...

Oh land, mine and afforested,
I am she, your daughter.
The woodlands and plains are singing.
The river and I combine our notes
into one Gypsy hymn.
I will go into the mountains
in a beautiful swinging skirt
made of flower petals.
I shall cry out with all my strength ...

My land, you were in tears,
you were pierced with pain,
My land, you cried in your sleep
like a small Gypsy child
hidden in the moss.
Forgive me, my land,
for my poor song
for its Gypsy strains.
Place your body against mine, my land.
When all is over, you will receive me.

Extracted from an article by J. Ficowski in Interpress Publishing

1574	**Portugal** Wearing of Romani dress banned.
1579	**Wales** First record of Gypsies.
1580	**Finland** First Roma reported on the mainland.
1584	**Denmark and Norway** Expulsion of the Roma ordered.
1586	**Belarus** Nomadic Roma expelled.
1589	**Denmark** Death penalty imposed for Roma not leaving the country.
1611	**Scotland** Three Gypsies hanged (under 1554 law).
1633	**Spain** Pragmatica of Felip IV. Expulsion.
1637	**Sweden** Death Penalty for Gypsies not leaving the country.
1714	**Scotland** Two female Gypsies executed.
1715	**Scotland** Ten Gypsies deported to Virginia.
1721	**Austro-Hungarian Empire** Emperor Karl VI orders the extermination of Roma throughout his domain.
1728	**Holland** Last Roma hunted down.

1746 **Spain**
Gypsies to live only in named towns.

1748 **Sweden**
Foreign Roma expelled.

1749 **Spain**
Round-up and imprisonment of all Roma ordered.

1758 **Austro-Hungarian Empire**
Maria Theresa begins assimilation program.

Son of the invisible people

Alexian Santino Spinelli (Italy)

father

      drops of milk red with blood
      gush from the diseased breast
      they sour the palate, revolt the appetite

father

      white snow, cold frost
      descends from a violent sky
      covering black skin with heat

father

      the horse, the wounded horse,
      gallops gaining no winning-posts
      its foaming sweat transformed to sour milk

father

      putrefying feet warming in the mud
      battering rains like wild nettles
      scourge the twisted back

father

      in the frozen night all the earth trembles
      the shrieking throat of the dusty violin
      echoes in the distance

father

      sleepless wind tugs at the hair
      hate-blackened moon blinds

father

      the hoarse song of plucked birds
      on desiccated olive twigs
      torments eternal rest

father

      the sun, the sun red with fire
      is a blazing ball
      it dries the smile wet with tears

father

 Romani song is repeating lamentation
 it comes forward, labours and dances
 sweet prolonged pain

father

 lightning like fiery knives
 comes down ruthlessly
 rending the famished belly

father

 the salt sea drowns, wise poverty
 flounders, eyes of wood are transfixed
 by images of cities already dead

father

 rivers of sobbing tears
 sweep away arcane melodies
 storms wash over our fraught nakedness

father

 infinite darkness bears light and justice
 in equal measure
 mute silence speaks of perpetual love

father

 grant me a glance of one who does not want to see
 that I may fade forever, completely dissolved,
 enfolded with the invisible people.

Translated from Italian by Sinéad ní Shuinéar

1759 Russia
Gypsies banned from St. Petersburg.

1763 Holland
Pastor Vályi is the first European to learn of the Indian origin of the Romani people.

The Gypsy from India

by Nicolas Jimenes Gonzalez (Spain)

I go looking for Gypsies
in the olive grove
because I was told
they were turned into dogs.

I am an Indian Gypsy woman
and learned from *Kali*[1]
the justice of logic,
the romance of magic.

I predicted your futures
throughout the centuries.
I developed the cures
for your sick mules and donkeys.

You never noticed me
as if it was madness
that drew money from
your fine young ladies.

But the time has come
to honour my people,
and free them from
the evil spell that I will

break with the spell I make.
They won't be dogs any more,
they will be what they were,
they will return to being the Roma –
Gypsies, as you would say.

Translated from Spanish by Tom Fugalli

---

[1]   Indian Goddess

1763	**Austro-Hungarian Empire**
	Székely Von Doba first brings Pastor Vályi's findings about the Indian origins of the Roma to academic attention in the November 6 edition of *The Vienna Gazette*.
1765	**Austro-Hungarian Empire**
	Joseph II continues assimilation program.
1782	**Hungary**
	Two hundred Roma are charged with cannibalism.

As the pelicans

by Béla Osztojkán (Hungary)
– For Károly Bari –

When neither sea, nor earth,
nor the depths of the forest
has enough food to offer
as the pelicans die
in times of great famine
so shall we die
and with the final heartache
of our last volition
we shall rip open our own claws
and to appease the insatiable hunger
of our starved comrades
we shall die
while feeding on ourselves
in small chunks
as the pelicans feed
numbed by the forest
and all that will remain after us
will be what we in our great pain
have most beautifully sung
in the moment of our death
as the pelicans sing
in the ear of the stifling night.

1783

Germany
Heinrich Grellmann publishes the first academic work establishing the Indian origin of the Romani people.

Spain
Romani language and dress banned.

United Kingdom
Most legislation against Gypsies repealed.

1802

France
Roma in Basque province rounded up and imprisoned.

1812

Finland
Order to confine nomadic Gypsies in workhouses.

1822

United Kingdom
Turnpike Act introduced: Gypsies camping on the roadside to be fined.

1830

Germany
Authorities in Nordhausen remove Roma children from their families for fostering with non-Roma.

1835

Denmark
Travellers hunted down in Jutland.

United Kingdom
Highways Act strengthens the provisions of the 1822 Turnpike Act.

1848

Transylvania
Emancipation of serfs.

1849

Denmark
Roma allowed in the country again.

1855

Romania
Emancipation of Romani slaves in Moldavia.

1856

Romania
Emancipation of Romani slaves in Wallachia.

1860

Sweden
Immigration restrictions eased.

1864 Romania
Final post-emancipation laws against Roma are rescinded, allowing them to own land.

1868 Holland
New immigration of Gypsies.

Richard Liebich's work on Roma introduces the phrase "lives unworthy of life" with specific reference to them, and later used as a racial category against Roma in Nazi Germany.

1872 Belgium
Foreign Roma expelled.

1874 Ottoman Empire
Muslim Roma given equal rights with other Muslims.

1875 Denmark
Roma barred from the country once more.

1879 Hungary
National conference of Roma in Kisfalu.

Serbia
Nomadism forbidden.

1884 Sweden
Dr. Kavalasky, a Romni, is appointed Professor of Mathematics at Stockholm University, the first female professor in Scandinavia.

1886 Bulgaria
Nomadism forbidden.

Germany
Bismarck recommends expulsion of foreign Roma.

c1890 Germany
A conference on "The Gypsy Scum" is held in Swabia, following Bismarck's anti-Romani position.

1899 Germany
Police Gypsy Information Service set up in Munich by Dillmann, later renamed "The Central Office for Fighting the Gypsy Nuisance."

Ode to the Twentieth Century

by Leksa Manuš (Latvia)

Twentieth Century,
What did you hold in store for the sad Roma people?
Did you bring the sun into our dark lives?
Did you dry the tears from our women's eyes?
Did you lighten our songs and dances with joy?

Twentieth Century: listen to our songs.
Can you hear from the notes
how our hearts have been drowned in tears?
Look at our dances:
Our women's steps may seem as light as a bird's,
but in reality they are trying
to cast off a bitter burden

from their aching shoulders.

That burden is you,
Twentieth Century,
and the sorrow you brought
into each of our lives.

1904 Germany
Prussian Parliament unanimously adopts proposal to regulate Gypsies' movements and work.

1905 Germany
A census of all Roma in Bavaria is taken.

1906 France
Identity cards introduced for nomads.

Germany
The Prussian minister issues special instructions to the police to "combat the Gypsy nuisance".

1907 Germany
Many Roma leave for other countries in Western Europe.

1910 Belgium
Django Reinhardt, famous jazz/blues guitarist, born to Romani family in a caravan near Ouchie.

Django

by Sandra Jayat (France)
– to my Gypsy brothers & sisters –

Django
Who would you be
if you were not
Django?

Like us
you are a true Gypsy –
but you are the greatest

Django
Your guitar strums in our heads
your music gives us hope
of living in freedom
and grants us the right of the city

Django
When you wander along the roads
bronze-skinned as a summer night
the river stirs
turns to velvet
and dreams of swallowing
the stream that runs at your feet.
Birds on the twigs
pick out
your next blues

Django
Like us
you have no king
no set of rules
but you have a mistress:
Music

Django
When jasmine blossoms in the air
of the manor of your dreams
you hasten to your caravan

Django
The Gypsy star
came looking for you
followed by an angel
carrying your guitar
to make a cloud of music
around Sarah

Django, Django
Music is raining blood
upon the earth.
Thousands of reeds
repeat your name:
Django

Translated from French by Ruth Partington

1914 Norway
Some thirty Roma are given Norwegian nationality.

Sweden
Deportation Act makes immigration of Roma difficult.

1918 Holland
Caravan and House Boat Law introduces controls over
movements of nomads.

1919 Bulgaria
Istiqbal (*Future*), a Romani organization, founded.

1920 Germany
Binding and Hoche publish their treatise on "Lives Unworthy of
Life" which targets Roma and uses the phrase first coined by
Liebich in 1868.

1922 Germany
In Baden all Roma are to be photographed and fingerprinted.

1923 Bulgaria
Journal *Istiqbal* (*Future*) commenced publication.

1924 Slovakia
A group of Roma are tried for cannibalism. They are found
innocent.

1925 USSR
All-Russian Union of Gypsies established.

1926 Germany
Bavarian state parliament brings in a new law "to combat Gypsy
nomads and idlers."

Switzerland
Pro Juventute starts a program of forced removal of travellers'
children from their families for fostering.

Extracts from:

A red foundling strolls into this dream

by Mariella Mehr (Switzerland)

i found
my body
on red velvet

for a long time
i'd roamed
toward this mountain

toward the black
pain at
the body's core

* * *

fear

(between title and
text – an empty trench
also called paragraph break)

naked
red-spiked openings
icebergs
that merge
over flowers

vanishing point

black space
devouring me

* * *

wedges of fire have driven
themselves into my brain
i've turned thorn-rose
temporarily

brimful red cup
bitter honey

i've carried myself
across the river of fire
as the brand of
a wayfarer's broken staff
remembering evaporated words

a bluebird
singed its wings
when learning to fly
with eyes
unprotected
i've drunken laughter
found abysses
they were black
but finite

with time's legs
around me
i've searched for
that one abyss

where your rainbow (b)looms for me

* * *

estranged from my shadow
i see it disappear with a snicker
into the winking eye of the elf

into the no-man's-sphere of the ancient days –

~

to gather all the deaths
to feel at home in the round of graves
and the hand that rolls my brain into silence
feels like rock –

quarries of words grow upward in time
into fossils of placeless
hopes

~

painless

* * *

at the end
of the world
my child screamed
a last scream
back into the
rainbow

a smell
of decaying eyes
in the socket of my hand

* * *

night face

in the dark
wolf's belly
are my other stars

hoarfrost ate up
the great
moon

lonely
colours fall
toward day

Translated from German by Anika Weiss

1926	**USSR** First moves to settle nomadic Roma.
1927	**Germany** Legislation requiring the photographing and fingerprinting of Roma instituted in Prussia. Bavaria institutes laws forbidding Roma to travel in large groups or to own firearms. **Norway** The Aliens Act bars foreign Roma from entering the country.
1928	**Germany** Nomadic Roma in Germany are to be placed under permanent police surveillance. Professor Hans F. Gunther writes that it was the Gypsies who introduced foreign blood into Europe.

Justice

Alexian Santino Spinelli (Italy)

Distant Indian blood
that irrigates Italic veins
never fed by the word
that regulates people
peoples and peoples that you,
you mixed together,
you dumped into the rivers
of our fathers from time
past,
and furrows and streams
you filled with tears
of honest women.
Winding through the highest minds
the Romani sentiment grew
murmuring the best words
to your young sons
and reaching the heart
of eternity.
Inhuman indifference annuls
and cries out loud
the simple word
that the fanatic mob kept hidden
and that you,
blood of my blood,
never knew!

Translated from Italian by Minna Proctor

1928 Slovakia
Pogrom in Pobedim.

1929 USSR
Pankov's Romani book *Buti I Džinaiben* (*Work and Knowledge*) published.

Journal *Romani Zorya* (*Romany Dawn*) starts publication.

1930 USSR
The first number of the Romani journal *Nevo Drom* (*New Way*) appears.

Give me a string to play on

by Djura Makhotin (Russia)

Oh, my life is like a silver mirror
The years are its frame.

I cannot see the time ahead
And what has passed I have forgotten.
In youth it seems that every day is long,
When one is older a year is like the breadth of a finger.
I am not guilty but I know the truth,
The road of life leads me.
I am not sad, I swear an oath, give me a string to play on.

May all my troubles leave me,
Let them fly away like birds.
The Roma travel under the sky to seek a deeper place.
We had clouds the day before yesterday,
Today the sun is golden.

Translated from Romani by Donald Kenrick and Valdemar Kalinin.

Ars poetica

by Andro Loleshtye (former USSR)

The fortune-tellers know, I don't,
how we should live, and how die.
I am a Rom, I just sing,
sing until the leaves fall down.

Translated by Leksa Manuš

Minarets of grass

by Dezider Banga (Slovak Republic)

I walked through the meadow
through the ink-black night
where the stars scorch:
that way led the poet's path.
In the suns' golden footsteps
where the forest bells ring
and the cool, still water whispers:
that way led the poet's path.
Where music is heard
great music,
a woodland symphony:
that way led the poet's path.
Where he sings of burning grief
of burdens carried by rocks:
that way led the poet's path.
Where the minarets of grass
pray in tongues of the *gadjé*
that way led the poet's path.

Austria

Officials in Burgenland call for the withdrawal of all civil rights of the Roma.

Bulgaria

Romani journal *Terbie* (*Education*) starts publication.

Germany

The National Socialist Party comes to power.
Measures against Gypsies and Jews begin:

- Roma musicians barred from State Cultural Chamber.

- Hitler's cabinet passes a law against the propagation of "lives unworthy of life", resulting in sterilizations and specifically aimed at "Gypsies and most of the Germans of black colour".

- Sinto boxer Johann Trollmann is stripped of his title as light-heavyweight champion for 'racial reasons'.

- "Beggars' Week" is instituted in which many Roma are arrested.

Seeing if there's something that makes me good for nothing

by José Heredia Maya (Spain)

Mother of the Spirit,
I am a Gypsy.
I don't have a bed
because I'm unlucky.

The best way to beg
is one that's discreet.
One must discover
the proper technique.

I saw a bishop
and a beggar,
only the former
was undercover.

The bishop's hat
is his disguise,
he passes it round
and promises the sky.

I am a Gypsy
and I am good,
but in the winter
I am cold.

Mother of the Spirit,
I was born a Gypsy.
Maybe there's something
that's wrong with me.

Translated from Spanish by Tom Fugalli

I'll sell you my tears

by Matéo Maximoff (France)

I'll sell you my tears.
If it is true I'm still small,
my heart is big.
If it is true I'm still a child,
I hurt like an adult.
Other children my age love each other, they play.
But I have to cry.
And since I possess nothing else
I will sell you my tears.
I see the children around me –
they don't have tears to sell,
their tears of pain
fall to the ground
and mix with the mud.
I take the tears from my cheeks,
and sell them to people who don't know how to cry.
But how much can I ask for them,
if I can't ask for consolation?
And if someone loves me,
I won't sell him my tears,
I will give them away,
for then they will be tears of joy.

Translated from Italian by Minna Proctor

1933 Romania

General Association of the Gypsies of Romania founded.
National conference held. Journals *Neamul Ţiganesc*
(*Gypsy Nation*) and *Timpul* (*The Time*) founded.

USSR

Teatr Romen, a Romani theatre company, performs the opera
Carmen, whose tragic heroine is a Gypsy.

1934 Germany

Gypsies who cannot prove German nationality expelled.

1935 Germany

Marriages between Gypsies and Germans banned; Gypsies
become subject to "The Nuremburg Laws for the Protection of
German Blood and German Honour".

Yugoslavia

Journal *Romano Lil* published.

1936 Germany

The right to vote removed from the Roma.

Opening of internment camp at Marzahn.

General Decree for fighting the Gypsy menace issued.

Racial Hygiene and Population Biological Research Unit of the
Health Office begins its work.

The Minister of War orders that Gypsies should not be called up
for active service.

I was born in black suffering

by Šaban Iliaz (Republic of Macedonia)

Oh yes, that's me all right
tramping along the road
barefoot, ravenous –
and on bad days
the wind blows
rain pours
and there's nowhere for me to shelter ...

> *Why did you bring me in the world, mother dear?*
> you bore me to a life of black suffering
> maybe you gave birth to me on a dark road like this
> my lips tremble, rain soaks me through
> and there's not even you, dear mother, to see me.

1938   ## Germany

April: Decree on the Preventative Fight against Crime issued in which all Roma are classified as antisocial. Many Roma are arrested and sent for forced labour to build concentration camps.

June 12-18: "Gypsy Clean-Up Week": hundreds of Sinti and Roma throughout Germany and Austria are rounded up, brutalized, and incarcerated: the beginning of the *Porrajmos* (Gypsy Holocaust).

Autumn: Racial Hygiene Research Centre begins to set up an archive of the Gypsy peoples. National Centre for Fighting the Gypsy Menace established.

December: Order for the "Fight against the Gypsy Menace". First mention of "The Final Solution of the Gypsy Question" in a document signed by Himmler.

USSR

Stalin bans Romani language and culture.

1939   ## Germany

Deportation of 30,000 Gypsies planned.

Settlement Decree is issued preventing Roma from travelling.

Gypsy fortune tellers arrested and sent to Ravensbrück concentration camp.

Poland

Special identity cards for Gypsies.

(German-occupied) Czech lands

Nomadism forbidden.

1940   ## France

French government opens internment camps for nomads.

Germany/Lands under German occupation

January: The first mass genocidal action of the Holocaust takes place in Buchenwald, when 250 Romani children are used as guinea-pigs to test the Zyklon-B gas crystals.

I remember a child

by Paola Schöpf (Italy)

I remember a child
Who thought this was a small world with a giant heart
Then he questioned the moon with his eyes
He believed that tears, screams, songs were carried off by the wind
Only to decorate his dwelling with new music

I remember a child
Who felt the sadness in the water and the moaning of the wind
Falling on the snow in the night with no tomorrow
And when he smiled there was sun in his eyes
He used a little mirror to reflect life, a prisoner of time

Then they came from the shadows like black butterflies
Four knights on white horses who decreed
Death because he was guilty of having been born
No one saw them
The passage of death was quick and silent
In the little campground

A torturous cry rent the white veil in the sky
The torturous cry of a skull that still would want to be kissed

I have embroidered that memory into my heart
That still little body now so far away from the hate and the anger
Alone and unarmed against death
I thought of his mouth full of dirt
Of his mouth full of regret for having believed in a world with
Giant heart
Eyes
Mouth
Unripe fruit returned to the earth

In a tiny hand the feeble lightshafts of a moon clustered
The Roma came, a gathering of silent hearts
The old mothers stood immobile, watching
The confused dogs observing the anguish of a foolish world

I remember a child
Roses spurting from his mouth
And two black eyes without life turned towards the sky
Like a mute prayer
Prayer for justice
Prayer for peace
Prayer for forgiveness

Translated from Italian by Minna Proctor

1940 — Germany/Lands under German occupation (continued)

April: Himmler orders the resettlement of Gypsies in the General Government of Poland.

August: Internment camp built at Maxglan, Slazburg, Austria. Labour camps set up in Lety and Hodonín in Czech lands.

October: Order for the internment of the Gypsies in Burgenland, Austria.

November: Internment camp for Gypsies is set up in Lackenbach, Austria.

1941 — Croatia

Jasenovac concentration camp opened.

Czech lands

In *August*, authorities decide that Gypsies from the so-called Protectorate are to be sent to a concentration camp.

Germany

March: Exclusion of Roma children from schools begins.

July: SS Chief Himmler's deputy Heydrich, chief architect of the Final Solution, announces that the Einsatzkommandos have "received the order to kill all Jews, Gypsies and mental patients".

Poland

A Gypsy camp is set up in the Jewish ghetto of Lodz for 5,000 inmates.

Serbia

German Military Command order states: Gypsies will be treated as Jews. In November, it further orders the immediate arrest of all Gypsies and Jews, who are to be held as hostages.

Slovakia

Decree on the Organization of the Living Conditions of the Gypsies. They are to be separated from the majority population.

1941

USSR/Baltic States

June: SS Task Forces move into the occupied areas of the Soviet Union and systematically kill Roma and Jews.

August: All the Sinti Gypsy families who lived in the Volga Republic are deported to Kazakhstan.

September: SS Task Force carry out mass executions of Roma and Jews in the Baby Yar valley.

December: Task Force C murders 824 Gypsies in Simferopol.

December: All the 101 Gypsies in the town of Libau, Latvia, are executed.

December: State Governor Lohse orders that Gypsies in Baltic States should be given the same treatment as Jews.

Yugoslavia

In *October*, German army executes 2,100 Jewish and Gypsy hostages (as a reprisal for soldiers killed by partisans).

1942

Bulgaria

Compulsory labour for Gypsies introduced.

Croatia

In *May*, the government and the Ustashi police issue the order to arrest all Gypsies and deport them to the extermination camp in Jasenovac.

Only ashes remain

by Bairam Haliti (Croatia)

They come from far flung places –
men, women, children,
hungry, dry, unshod –
They are the Roma,
dressed in rags,
walking through mud.

They are drawn by
promises of a land
they can call their own,
houses, fields, firesides:
false Ustashi words.

They are a people of sorrow.

Only a chamber of gas
awaits them.
Their infants are screaming,
all sleep forsaken.
Their land is a mound
of charred limbs.

Where once there were
dreams,
white horses,
distant plains,
only ashes remain.
The innocent child's smile
has evaporated into sky.

Czech lands

6,500 Gypsies registered by the police on one day in August.

Germany

March: A special additional income tax is levied on Gypsies.

July: A decree of the General Staff of the Army orders that Gypsies are not to be taken for active military service.

September: Himmler and Justice Minister Thierack agree to transfer any Gypsies in prison to concentration camps.

December: Himmler issues the order to deport the Gypsies in Greater Germany to the concentration camp of Auschwitz-Birkenau.

Poland

January: All Sinti and Roma from the Lodz ghetto are transported and gassed at Chelmo.

April: Roma are brought into the Warsaw ghetto and kept in the prison in Gesia street.

May: All Roma in the Warsaw district are to be interned in Jewish ghettoes.

July: Several hundred Polish Roma killed at Treblinka extermination camp.

Romania

Some 20,000 Roma are deported to Transdnistria.

Serbia

German Minister Dr. Turner announces in August that "the Gypsy question has been fully resolved".

Germany

Several hundred Gypsy prisoners start work on the production of the V1 and V2 weapons in underground workshops in Kohnstein Hills.

1943 Poland

January: Roma from Warsaw ghetto transferred to the extermination camp at Treblinka.

February: First transports of Sinti and Romani from Germany are delivered to the new Gypsy Section in Auschwitz Birkenau.

March: In Auschwitz the SS gas some 1,700 Romani men, women and children.

May: SS Major Dr. Josef Mengele is transferred at his own request to Auschwitz-Birkenau concentration camp.

July: Himmler visits the Gypsy Section in Auschwitz and orders the Roma to be killed.

USSR

Minister for the Occupied Eastern Territories proclaims that all nomadic Gypsies in the territories are to be treated as Jews.

1944 Belgium

In *January*, a transport of 351 Roma and Sinti from Belgium is despatched to the Auschwitz-Birkenau concentration camp.

Holland

In *May*, a transport of 245 Roma and Sinti is sent to Auschwitz concentration camp.

The terror years

by Rajko Djurić (Yugoslav Republic/Germany)

Our house is Auschwitz,
So big and black. So black and big.
Petals of skull are hidden,
Strewn amidst the tall grass.
Prayers rise up and fall back
Beneath the ashes, beneath the dreams,
Searching for a door, a road out.

House so big. House so black.
Lightless house, hopeless house.

As I arrive at our house
My lips turn blue.
These terror years are my path;
Their names are the way-stations.

Our house is Auschwitz,
So big and black. So black and big.
This is where our tears flow,
Destroying our sight.
This is where they crushed our pleas
For no one to hear.
This is where they turned us to ashes
For the winds to scatter.

Listen, Adam! Listen, Simon!
Eve and Mary, too!
The twenty-five thousand shadows
That watch and follow me:
These terror years are our path;
Their names are the way-stations.

House so big. House so black.
House with no street, house with no address.

Translated from French by Julie Ebin

A wedding in Auschwitz

by Rajko Djurić (Yugoslav Republic/Germany)

– There's Ari! Ari! Don't you see my brother Ari?

– No. All I see is a big yellow butterfly. I see a butterfly, but not your brother Ar...

– That is my brother Ari! It's not a butterfly! I swear on my life that I'm telling the truth.

– I don't agree to such risky and dangerous criteria of truth. But let's not talk about life and truth. How do you know that this yellow butterfly is your brother?

– How do I know? I see his face, his nose, his eyes, his hair. I know that the human mind is a moral acrobat, but my eyes have never fooled me. I see it as I did back then, how he takes desperate breaths as though he breathed in death itself. No one in Auschwitz breathed like him! He breathed with his eyes and ears, reached for the air with his hands, like a drowning man for a straw. And while he breathed I thought I heard a symphony. Today I still hear his breathing, life and death struggling in it, like a concert at which Mozart's Requiem and Beethoven's Ninth resound at the same time. Just listen! All of Auschwitz is resonating!

– I can really hear something. But I don't know what it is. First it sounds like raging demons, then like a choir of angels. Hold on, now it's neither one nor the other, but something like the voices of newborn children... No, that's impossible! I have to rid myself of these illusions in order to define it.

You're right. We have to rid ourselves of illusions and face the truth. Just as I'm facing you. Now I will tell you something that I once couldn't believe because it seemed like a hallucination to me. Over there where that stone has been erected, there used to be the "Black Horologist Shop." That was the out-patient room of Dr. Kiss. He examined children and often adults as well. I, too, went to him. On the walls of his room were different clocks, from the very smallest to the largest. That's why the shack was also called "Black Horologist Shop." Some worked like hourglasses but instead of sand or water they contained the blood of children, men and women, lymph, crushed human tissue. I was told that Dr. Kiss used to be a passionate collector of clocks. When he came to Auschwitz he started to build clocks using the blood and the organs of people. It was said that he even intended to construct clocks from human genes. I don't know how much of this is true, but I did see with my own eyes a clock made of a child's skeleton. At noon the skeleton would open up, the heart would peek out, and a sound like children's laughter could be heard. This would be repeated three times, then the skeleton would close, and the clock would go on ticking like before. Once Dr. Kiss said to me: "If you don't obey you will soon keep this clock company and join it in a ticking duet." That's why I hate clocks! I have never worn a watch on my wrist or had a clock at home. When I see a clock, I'm looking death in the face. Death and Dr. Kiss.

I have to tell you something else: Dr. Kiss had a big German Shepherd called Rex. The food we were fed was prepared according to the recipes of the Auschwitz kitchen (sometimes I have this idea to write an "Auschwitz Cookbook" because I've noticed that literature on food and drinks is very popular in Germany. When eating "à la Auschwitz" people would better understand some things. I'm just afraid that someone – God forbid! – might open a restaurant called "Auschwitz" and it would be my fault). Rex was served meals worthy of a king. When I walked past him once I caught the smell of real meat. Rex growled at me so terrifyingly that I thought he would tear my heart to pieces. When he ate, it seems to me, he would not tolerate the shadow of a bird or a leaf near him. After my brother Ari's death I went over to Rex one evening. Fear had withered inside me like grass in the desert. I went over to Rex and said: "Ari!" Rex looked at me – I thought I saw tears in his eyes. Then he put his tail between his legs and left. I grabbed the meat with both hands and devoured it like the Jews when they found the manna. Ever since that day Rex was my friend. I believed he had changed because Ari's soul had entered him. Who knows what had happened?

By the way, as long as the ways of the Lord are a mystery to man, the ways of the soul are also shrouded in mystery. To give you an example, I don't know what happens to you when you dream of your father and mother, but when my parents appear to me in a dream I know that on the following day the devil will touch me with his tail, even if I try to take refuge in God's house! Particularly so, when I dream of my mother Kali . These dreams seem to throw a "switch" inside me, and suddenly I see all the dangers threatening me at that moment. Every person probably has that "switch" inside, which will be activated in his dreams, but only by the hands or the breath of those whose genes he carries and who have planted the strongest and purest love in his heart. If I'm not mistaken, they're our "guardian angels".

You say that I'm a dreamer. Maybe you're right because when I reached Auschwitz I wasn't old enough to face life and death. But very soon I bore the language of death under my tongue and the experience of life on my tongue. Now I will tell you something that's neither dream nor reality, but really both at once. The evening before a wedding was to take place in Auschwitz, I dreamed that my mother Kali was sewing the gown for the bride. The barracks was full of flowers – from those that God created down to the small blue ones that grew under the barbed wire at Auschwitz. My mother would take blossom upon blossom, twirl them between her fingers, and they would come together all on their own. Once she had finished the gown, the kind worn by flamenco dancers, she held it against herself as if to try it on and asked me: "Do you like it?" My heart was filled with joy, I started to laugh and could not speak a word, I was laughing so hard. "So you like it," she said. To let her know that she was right I gave her a kiss. "That's the gown for the bride, that pretty Spanish woman, Dolores. She's getting married tomorrow. There'll be a wedding in Auschwitz! Bring her the dress and tell her that I will also have the bridal garland ready soon."

I took the dress and ran to the barracks where Dolores stayed. When she had put on the gown the barracks was transformed into the most beautiful church. The angels were singing. The bridegroom arrived, kissed her and said: "Hurry up. The Lord has come to wed us." They went to the altar. I heard only the echo of God's words. Then I, too, opened my mouth and sang along with the angels. And so for the first time I awoke singing in Auschwitz. But that day there really was a wedding in Auschwitz!

A wedding in Auschwitz? Is that possible? you ask, surprised.

Yes, there was a wedding in Auschwitz. But the bridegroom and bride were in striped uniforms. A Catholic priest wed them in the presence of officers wearing swastikas. Afterwards people ate and drank and danced to the music a little.

Who was the couple? you ask.

I can't tell you for sure. But my mother told me that they were Spaniards. The groom was tall and strong, the bride as small and delicate as a bird. I remember that the groom even sang a song, and my uncle Toka played the violin. A sad song – "Mama" was the only word I understood. Later several rumours about them went round: they were Communists, they were Nazi spies, they weren't really people but dolls that the Nazis had dressed up as bride and groom for their amusement. Some even said that they were really God's envoys who were supposed to explore how people lived in Auschwitz and what was happening on earth. To be quite honest, I also believed that God had sent them. Later other thoughts went through my mind: Where had they gone? What had they done? Who had they worked for? Those were thoughts like the devil who kicks with the left hoof one moment and with the right one the next! Perhaps I had these thoughts because of Rina whom I met at the wedding. I fell in love with her. She was a little older than I. And when she looked at me so sweetly that something was set in motion inside me. I felt the warm blood rise in my veins. After the wedding I met Rina two or three more times. Once snow was falling, so white, it couldn't have been whiter. She shivered with cold. To warm her up, I hugged and kissed her. That was my first kiss. Rina was as red as a rose! She ran away. Out of fear, embarrassment – I'm not sure. As she ran from me I looked after her, and it seemed to me as though from each of her footsteps in the snow roses were growing. When Rina had disappeared the entire field of snow was covered with red roses. If I had closed my eyes for good at that moment I could have said: God gave me a good death! But instead I just got sick. And now I'm so sick that life trickles out of me like the stinking straw from the plank bed I lie on. Everything hurts, there's three-dimensional pain in every particle of body and soul. But when my lids grow heavy I don't close them because I'm afraid I might not be able to open them again. When it dawns the pain eases up and I gather what little life I've left inside. Secretly, I feel whether my heart is still beating in my chest; with my tongue I check how many teeth my jaws are still holding; with my lower lip I heal the new sores on the upper lip and with the upper lip the old ones on the lower lip. I hold my left hand in my right hand, open it and examine my palm which looks like a cracked mirror pulled out of the grave. Once I was able to get up again, I had no choice but to line up for roll call outside. I walk, stagger, make it. I'm a crushed blade of straw that's burning, but I'm afraid of turning to ashes and of sweeping up my life with the broom of my being. They march across the grave that holds the grass and the children's shoes; their step is firm. And I think that the earth has flown up and the sky has fallen down.

On this desolate soil, where they and I are standing, I've thought a hundred times: this is the end. You watch over your life, but death is perched on your shoulder, creeps into you through the ears and nostrils, settles on the eye lids, creeps through the eyelashes and across the brow like a worm, and once it reaches the temples a mortal sweat starts to flow on your skin and inside you. Everything is dead: your hair is falling out, your skin is tearing, your lips are swollen and scabby, your teeth loose in their festering jaws, your ears seem to be filled with stale water, your lids are heavier than lead, your pupils stare, your tongue is dry, your saliva dried up, your lungs hurt with every breath, your heart is bleeding, your body burning, hurting when you urinate; when you lift up a leg you risk falling. Everything is dead, everything except the fear that's creeping through the web of your veins, straining the nerves and tearing your soul to shreds.

Translated from German by Anika Weiss

1944 Poland

On August 2, a night to be remembered as *Zigeunernacht* (*Gypsy Night*), 1,400 Romani prisoners are sent from Auschwitz to Buchenwald concentration camp. The same night the remaining 2,900 Roma are killed in the gas chamber.

Slovakia

Roma join the fight of partisans in the Slovak National Uprising.

1945 Poland

On January 27 at 3pm the first Soviet soldiers reach the main camp at Auschwitz and find one Rom among the survivors.

Europe

May: World War II ends in Europe. All surviving Roma freed from camps.

Bulgaria

Romani Organization for the Fight against Fascism and Racism set up.

Germany

Nuremburg Trials of Nazi leaders begin. Crimes against Gypsies are included in the charges.

1946 Poland

Roma Ensemble founded.

1947 Bulgaria

Theater Roma in Sofia established.

1951 Bulgaria

Theater Roma in Sofia closed.

1953 Denmark

Roma readmitted to the country.

1958 **Bulgaria**
Nomadism banned.

Czechoslovakia
Nomadism banned.

Hungary
Romani organization established.

1960 **England and Wales**
Caravan Sites Act reduces provision of caravan sites.

The wooden rose

by Hester Hedges (England)

And we all shared a summer:

She and I, we worked
the fields in common years.
For me, the sun still
brings warmth and light.
But not for her.

The field, a pleasant walk,
its stillness silencing our idle chat,
found us lazy, sat on hay,
or under trees
that sheltered us
from rain and shadowed sun.

They stand still,
witnesses of
her lavender lips,
resting by clouds.
And the end of every evening
song brought new meaning
to old words.

Until it happened –

Quite quickly it seemed to me,
the idiot I am, who now can only just
remember
how that summer died ...
Our people travelled far
when fields were bare
and mornings late.
I watched her life fold away,
the water churning and
empty fruit baskets
stacked higher
than my castles in the sky.

Mounted lines of moving horses
took her off for winter
with nothing left behind,
no gift for us to keep
lest we forget –

Only a wooden rose,
carved by those tiny fingers:
it lies undisturbed upon the steep
amid the dried plants
taken from a summer's breeze
and scattered far and wide.

When a new haze decides to come
I take out my wooden promise
and look at the days that quickly went
sleeping on a bed of heather.

1962

German Federal Republic
Courts rule that Roma were persecuted for racial reasons.

Norway
Government Gypsy Committee set up.

1963

Ireland
Report of the Commission on Itinerancy published.

Italy
Opera Nomadi education scheme set up.

1966

Britain
Gypsy Council set up.

1967

Finland
Gypsy Association established.

1968

Council of Europe
Rudolf Karway, President of the Ziguenermission, a civil rights movement based in Hamburg, leads a delegation to the Human Rights Commission in Strasbourg.

Holland
All districts must build caravan sites.

England and Wales
Caravan Sites Act. Councils to build sites.

1969

Bulgaria
Segregated schools are set up for Roma.

Council of Europe
Assembly passes a positive resolution on Roma.

1970

United Kingdom
National Gypsy Education Council established.

1971

England
First World Romani Congress held near London.

Scotland
Advisory Committee on the Travelling People starts work.

1972

Czechoslovakia
Sterilization programme for Roma begins.

England
Romani Guild founded.

1972 Sweden
Stockholm's Finska Zigenarförening founded.

1973 German Federal Republic
Three Roma shot by farmer in Pfaffenhofen.

Scandinavia
Nordiska Zigenarrådet to link organizations.

Yugoslavia
Macedonia. Radio broadcasts in Romani start from Tetovo.

1975 Council of Europe
Committee of Ministers passes a positive resolution on nomads.

Hungary
Magazine *Rom Som* (*I am a Romani*) starts appearing.

1977 England and Wales
Cripps Report on Gypsies published.

Holland
Legalization of 500 "illegal" Roma immigrants.

United Nations
Sub-commission resolution on protection of Roma.

1978 Switzerland
2nd World Romani Congress in Geneva.

1979 Hungary
National Gypsy Council formed.
First national exhibition of self-taught Romani artists.

Norway
ABC Romani primer produced for mother tongue teaching.

United Nations
Romani Union recognized by ECOSOC.

1980 Yugoslavia
Romani Grammar in Romani published in Skopje.

1981 German Federal Republic
3rd World Romani Congress in Göttingen.

Poland
Pogrom in Oswiećim.

1981 **Yugoslavia**
Roma granted national status on an equal footing with other minorities.

1982 **France**
New Mitterand government promises to help nomads.

1983 **Italy**
Romani caravans removed from Rome at the start of the Annus Sanctus.

Northern Ireland
Belfast Traveller Education Development Group established.

Yugoslavia
Romani teaching begins in one school in Kosovo.

1984 **European Parliament**
Passes a resolution on aiding Roma.

1985 **England**
Bradford's attempts to make it illegal for nomadic Gypsies to come within city limits overthrown by the courts.

France
First International Exhibition (Mondiale) of Romani Art in Paris.

Ireland
Report of the Travelling People Review body published.

Sweden
Attack on a Romani family in Kumla with stones and a fire-bomb.

1986 **France**
International Romani conference in Paris.

Spain
Romani houses set on fire in Martos.

Yugoslavia
International Romani seminar in Sarajevo.

1987 **U.S.**
The U.S. Holocaust Memorial Council appoints its first Rom member, seven years after its creation.

Up the chimneys

by Charlie Smith (England)

Up the chimneys went the Rom –
with them they thought their story gone.
The dust it flew around the earth,
in the rains it settled on turf;
although the smoke has now gone
in the wind you can hear their song.
By our youth now the story will be told,
the *Gorgios*[1] lies will then unfold
and the Gypsy flower grow more bold.

---

[1] Non-Gypsies

1989

Germany

Government initiates the deportation of several thousand foreign Roma from the country.

Roma demonstrate in the ex-concentration camp at Neuengamme against the deportation of asylum seekers.

Hungary

Roma Parliament set up.

Romania

Border guards shoot party of Roma.

Spain

Romani houses attacked in Andalusia.

1990

Poland

Permanent exhibition on Roma opens in Tarnow.

4th World Romani Congress held near Warsaw.

Standard alphabet for Romani adopted by World Romani Congress.

White snows fall on Belarus

by Valdemar Kalinin (Belarus)

Strong winds are rattling my window panes
It's pouring down by the ladle
But what weather reigns in my native plains?
Tell me, wind, if you're able.

White snows fall on Belarus, he answers,
The Roma, speaking Romani tongue,
Visit festivals on their horses.
– Then our forests are basking in sun.

Translated from Romani by Valdemar Kalinin

New Rom

by Jimmy Story (Australia)
– for Jozsef and Gustav –

Who are we,
Roma without Romanes
who must read
our own history
in another tongue,
follow the butterfly
of our own being
across maps of imagination
trying to recreate
the lost structure
of our soul?

We are your children.
You, who fought battles,
traded metal, horses,
dreams and tongues
in order to survive;
who told the Magnificent Lie
and ended up in chains
as galley slaves,
deportees
outlaws and brigands
in ashes and in lime.

If we learn Romanes
from books and not
our mother's breast
it is only because
the long cloak of assimilation
the rubber stamp of jackboots
and the mask of shame
almost destroyed
the butterfly's fragile wings.

If we travel in aeroplanes
rather than *vurdon*[1]
it is because
our journey has taken us
so far apart.

We read the future
from a fax machine
and not a crystal ball.

If we reconstruct history
from dust and ashes
it is because this dust
came from our own feet
and the ashes from our bones.

---

[1] caravan

I am the common Rom

by Gregory Dufunia Kwiek (USA/Poland)

Hello, I'm the common Rom.
When us Rom are organized and live in one area, that place is a *lageri.*[1]

Hello, I'm the common Rom.
Some fool told me to reveal to *gadjé* that I'm a Rom, and stand up –
(I don't think this guy was a Rom).

Hello, I'm the common Rom.
What do you mean, we are trash, the lowest of the low?
Then we probably deserve the way *gadjé* treat us.

Hello, I'm the common Rom.
How dare you say my *vitsa*[2] were once slaves?
Maybe yours were, but certainly not mine.
Maybe those slaves were the really *trashy* Gypsies.

Hello, I'm the common Rom.
Who's from India, you mad man?

Hello, I'm the common Rom.
Education? Are you joking?
We can't change – it's in our blood.
We will always be stupid Rom.

Hello, I'm the common Rom.
What do you mean, "listen to the *magerdo*[3] *gadjo*"?
Get out of my face!

Hello, I'm the common Rom.
Bow your head when the *gadjo* passes,
don't get him angry,
don't speak Romanes or he will recognise us.

Hello, I'm the common Rom.
What do you mean *sue*?
I just want to get out of this mess.
I'll leave this town without looking back.

Hello, I'm the common Rom.
Again they recognised us as Rom!
I told you kids not to speak Romanes in front of the *gadjé*.
Now it's time to move again.
And why did you go and wear a long skirt, girl?
The *gadjo* knew right away we were Rom;
now we'll never get an apartment.

---

[1] concentration camp
[2] clan
[3] unclean

1990 **Poland**
Journal *Rrom p-o Drom* (*Roma on the Road*) founded.

Romania
Miners attack Romani quarter in Bucharest.

1991 **Czech Republic**
Romani teaching starts at Prague University.

Macedonia
Roma accorded equal rights in new republic.

Poland
Pogram in Mlawa.

Ukraine
Police attack Romani settlement at Velikie Beryezni.

1992 **Hungary**
Arson attack on Roma in Kétegyháza.

Poland
Attack on Roma in Oswiećim.

Slovakia
Romathan Theater established in Kośice.

Ukraine
Mob attacks Romani houses in Tatarbunary.

United Nations
Commission on Human Rights passes resolution on protection of Roma.

1992 -1993 **Former Yugoslavia**
As war in the Balkans gathers pace, many Roma flee to avoid conscription. Others targeted by military on various sides.

The Bosnian tragedy

by Gjünler Abdula (Republic of Macedonia/Holland)
– for the People who died in the war –

Black clouds float about the multitudes
Suddenly the crowds have gone silent
For a dark time is unleased in Bosnia.
In all quarters is the clash of armaments
The war has begun: those who were brothers
Yesterday are mortal enemies today.

> The sound of *ezan*[1] comes no more from the mosques
> The minarets have been toppled
> The people have forgotten their God.

The schools are empty of children
Who cower instead in hiding places.
The machines in the factory are still
Men and women alike have armed themselves
And their blood flows in the street gutters
Feet, hands, arms, eyes, minds,
Everything is soiled in blood
Even infants, their hands in their mothers',
Have surrendered their souls to God.

> For how long will
> Death reign
> Anguish be routine
> Children scream
> Death be daily?
> Tell me how long
> You will dance
> This tragic dance.

Translated from Dutch by Peter Steentoft and Chris Dohmen

---

[1] call to prayer

1993

Austria
Indigenous Roma recognized as ethnic group.

Bulgaria
A crowd of Bulgarians attacks the Romani quarter in Malorad, killing one Romani man.

Czech Republic
Tibor Danihel, a young Rom, drowns running away from skinhead gang.

Seven Roma deported from Ústí nad Labem to Slovakia.

Hungary
International Conference in Budapest.

Macedonia
Official introduction of Romani language in schools.

Romania
Three Roma killed in pogrom in Hadareni.

Scotland
Scottish Gypsy Traveller Association set up.

Slovakia
Cyril Dunka, a Rom, beaten up by police after a parking incident.

United Nations
The International Romani Union petitions for and receives promotion to Category II, Special Consultative Status.

1994

Britain
Criminal Justice Act. Nomadism criminalised.

Hungary
Budapest OSCE meeting sets up "Contact Point for Roma and Sinti Issues" – to be based initially in Warsaw.

Roma vote for their local Romani councils.

1994

Poland

ODIHR organizes Warsaw seminar on Roma. Romani boy beaten up and houses inhabited by Roma attacked in Debica.

France

At a meeting in Strasbourg, the Standing Conference of Romani Associations is formed.

1995

Austria

Four Roma killed by a bomb in Oberwart, Burgenland.

Bulgaria

One Rom dies following an arson attack on a block of flats in Sofia. Angel Angelov, a Rom, shot by police in Nova Zagora.

Czech Republic

Tibor Berki, a Rom, killed by skinheads in Zdár nad Sázavou.

France

Council of Europe in Strasbourg sets up specialist advice group on the Roma.

Hungary

Second International Exhibition (Mondiale) of Romani Art.

Roma attacked and injured in Kalocsa.

Poland

Romani couple murdered in Pablanice.

Grota Bridge settlement of Romanian Gypsies in Warsaw is raided by police and its residents deported across the border to Ukraine.

The raid

by Alexian Santino Spinelli (Italy)

A knock on the door in the deepest night
the ferocious teeth of trained dogs
an automatic gun pointed at the sleepy face
shattered dream nightmarish hallucinations
black uniforms piercing stares
disgust and hate slanderous accusations
violent hurricane innocent eyes ...
the door closed a dream disappeared
tears on the ground ... torn hearts.

Translated from Italian by Minna Proctor

1995 Slovakia

Mario Goral, a Rom, burnt to death by skinheads in Žiar nad Hronom. Union of Romani Political Parties formed.

Inside me the wind howls

by Margita Reiznerová (Slovak Republic/Belgium)

Inside me the wind howls
Inside me a storm rages
And fills me so with rain
That it streams out from my eyes.
Inside me it thunders
And anger surges,
Beating on my heart
Like a hammer on an anvil.
Only my soul is pure
It beseeches, cries out,
Quelling the fury within me.

I close my eyes,
Press my hands together
And raise them up.
My mouth opens,
Words come out:
Listen!
I want to be good
I want to know the sun.

Translated from Romani by Burton Bollag

The apparition of Choxani[1]

by Luminiţa Mihai Cioabă (Romania)

I met her one night.
With a flower between her white teeth
She seemed a goddess then, through the darkness,
She was light.

And looking in her eyes
I saw sadness through and through,
And my gaze
Drowned in her tearful lashes.
I took her flower with a kiss.
She lifted star dust from her breast
And brushed it on my eyes.
Saying the magic word *kamavtu*[2],
She stretched toward me and took her flower
Returning to me my kiss.

And she disappeared into the night,
Taking my heart and my eyes.

And now, though I am alive, I taste death
Coursing through my body like a great river.
The forest swallowed her.
The mountain hid her.
The water covered her.
Maybe she was only a ghost.
She is hidden in me,
And she wants to touch my hand
Kiss my lips.

Translated from Italian by Minna Proctor

---

[1] Choxani is a witch who brings retribution to those
who stray away from the Romani culture

[2] Kamavtu is Romani for "I love you"

1995

Turkey
Zehala Baysal, a Rom, dies in police custody in Istanbul.

U.S
First national conference on the *Porrajmos* (*Romani Holocaust*) held at Drew University.

1996

Albania
Fatmir Haxhiu, a Rom, dies of burns after a racist attack.

Austria
Nicola Jevremovic, a Rom, and his wife beaten by police after a traffic incident.

Bulgaria
Kuncho Anguelov and Kiril Perkov, Romani deserters from the army, shot and killed by military police. Three Roma beaten up by skinheads in Samokov. Petra Stoyanova, another Rom, shot dead by police in Rakovski.

Czech Republic
Romani children banned from using swimming pool in Kladno.

European Court of Human Rights
The Court rejects the appeal by Mrs Buckley against the refusal of planning permission in England for her caravan.

France
Second Meeting of the Standing Committee of Romani Organizations and first meeting of the Committee of Experts of the Council of Europe in Strasbourg.

Greece
Police raid on Romani camp in Attica. Police officer shoots Anastasios Mouratis, a Rom, in Boetia.

Hungary
European Roma Rights Centre set up in Budapest.

Ireland
National Strategy on Traveller Accommodation proposed.

The stone

by Chrissie Ward (Ireland)

Author's note: This poem is about the boulders blocking every traditional
camping ground used by Travellers in the Republic of Ireland. The
authorities, by use of these stones, have left no camping space for the
Travellers and have forced the Travellers into houses as a way of getting
rid of both them and their traditions.

Take away the cruel stone
longer and larger than life
the black, dark stone
of envy, death and greed.
Everywhere you go
before you turn the wheel
it's the black stone you'll meet
driving you from light
taking over your life
ruling over your world
burying you deep.

Take away the stone
that holds back our freedom
killing the only life
we've ever had.
Envy-stone without a heart
cold and hard, no feelings has it
haunting us travellers every day.
A chain of black stones
around the green shamrock:

What once was ours
is no more.

The dark, black stones:
there's a curse upon them
from the prisoners of those stones.
So take away the stones
free our souls
let us live in light.
The black is the enemy
blocking our spirit
in the summer time
killing our freedom without a gun
ruling the hearts of everyone.

Born free, but light shines no more
the stones have locked the door
to the hearts of everyone.
Wish to be free
and take away the stones
that watch our wild Irish land
and let the travellers' spirit
the living and the dead
Be free again.

1996

Poland
Houses occupied by Roma attacked in Wiebodzice.

Romania
Twenty-one Romani houses burnt down in Curtea de Arges.

Mircea-Muresul Mosor, a Rom, shot and killed by the chief of police in Valcele.

Serbia
Attack on Roma in Kraljevo.

Extracts from:

Prayer of an impious father and Gypsy mother

by Rajko Djurić (Yugoslav Republic/Germany)

Dedicated to a boy who died, aged 2, in a Serbian village.
He died naturally, of a serious illness, but his burial was
anything but natural. It was a fight just to win him a burial
place. The boy was Rom ...

Devla barea[1]
How do you want me to pray?
How do you want me to say my say?
Tell me, god:
do you want it in Serbian –
or maybe Gypsy tongue?
You know well enough what I think:
it was your angel of death
carried off my son.

Do you want us to raise you up a church?
Do you want us to light some candles?
Devla zuralea[2]
It's you who holds all the keys:
return me my son.
I'll buy him some patent sandals
and a suit of white.
He died naked and unshod
he'll curse me, no doubt
and bring shame on you.

I'll sell my house
courtyard included
and even, if necessary,
the dirt in my fingernails –
anything to keep him happy.
He went hungry and thirsty.
You have your business to go about
so who will look after him? ...

---

[1] Great God
[2] Powerful God

Devla guglea[3]
Never before did I pray
three days
three nights
but what good are my words?
What is there left to say

when you can peer into my soul.
It's darker there, darker even
than your angel of death ...

Devla morrea[4]
If you have shut your house
open at least a grave
or let us dig a grave
a grave in the air.

Have pity, Lord,
return me my son.
I have brought him his sandals and his suit ...

Devlea karalea[5]
Bury then the father with the son
blow down my house
spit on my courtyard
or better still
piss on this village
that I might see your handiwork.
Then obliterate me into silence
efface the name of the dog
the name of the cock
that the name of the stone even
may be lost to oblivion
that I might see how they call us
"Gypsies".
Ah, do something
you blasted god
or leave me be the judge
Jertisar Devla[6]
I grow mad with injustice ...

---

[3] Sweet God
[4] My God
[5] Lustful God
[6] Forgive me, God

Devla barea[7]
It's now the sixth day.
Our impotency
is the measure of your
potency

Devla korrea
Karalea dilea
Devla...[8]

Lament of the mother

Dig brothers dig
dig a deep trench
cut out the ears
of the earth
so its cry can't be heard
expose the lungs
of the earth
so we can see its breath
Dig brothers dig
a deeper trench still
dig down to the bowels
of the earth
so I can enshroud
this wound of six days
this grief of six nights
Dig brothers dig
a trench deeper still
dig into me
with your black-eyed gaze
dig into me
and make of me his tombstone.

Translated from French by Siobhan Dowd

---

[7] Great God
[8] Blind God, Foolish God

1996

Slovakia
Jozef Miklos, a Rom, dies when his house is set on fire in Zalistie.

Spain
Romani Union's 2nd "Sarajevo" Peace Conference, in Vittoria.

Turkey
Five thousand evicted from Selamsiz quarter of Istanbul.

Ukraine
A Romani woman known as Mrs H. reportedly raped by police in Velikie Beryezni. Two brothers are also shot by police in the same town.

1997

January

Austria
Mr. and Mrs. Jevremovic given suspended prison sentences for "resisting arrest" (see 1996 above).

Hungary
Fine increased on appeal for the owner of an inn in Pecs who had discriminated against Roma.

Romania
Mob attacks Romani houses in Tananu village.

Ukraine
Roma beaten by police in four separate incidents in Uzhorod.

February

Bulgaria
Killing of three Roma by police reported. Police attack the Romani quarter in Pazardjik.

Czech Republic
Appeal Court in Pilsen quashes acquittal of inn owner Ivo Blahout on a charge of discrimination against Roma.

Hungary
Roma beaten up in police station in Szombathely and in a police car in Mandatany in a separate incident.

March

France
Jose Ménager and Manolito Meuche, two Roma, shot dead by police in Nantes.

My father, God be good to him

from: an oral memoir

by Chrissie Ward (Ireland)

I think me father was about thirty-six when he died. They say me father was murdered but there was nothing done about it because we were Travellers in the North and Irish people, they didn't like people from the South. So Travellers, they was kinda discriminated upon, and nobody ever made enquiries about it. So he was killed in a police station.

He was going up to see me mother one night in hospital. She was in hospital 'fore me sister was born. She was sick. He used to drive over and back to see her.

And coming back he used to push his bike, coming back. So he was coming back this night and the police just dragged him in. In the morning there was me older sister, about twelve she was, and the police came to her to identify his body. He was found dead. They left him all night swimming in blood in the police station and they say it was a haemorrhage in the brain. But he was healthy like, a really healthy man. But they say that's what killed him.

The last place I think I remember me father was at Kennedy's bakers on the Falls Road. We used to pull in in the winter and we used to move out in the summer. So that's me father, he used do the work for the settled people, and he used to deal with the settlers, and we'd kinda pull in if the women was having a baby or something just to be near at hand to a hospital and that was in a Catholic area. It was mostly Catholic areas – I think the Travellers used to kinda camp in the poorer areas – and that's the last place I remember when me father was alive.

It was always, funny enough, dawn, always dawn in the morning when you'd be in bed when They'd come. Come and beat the top o' the tent. They were very cruel, the north police, they was very cruel to Travellers because they didn't like them. Now a lot o' them were sons of the B Specials. And they always used to beat the top o' the tent very, very hard and they'd say, Get up out that yiz... What's that they use' ta call us? Ye Dirty Gippos. Get up outa that. And we wouldn't get up. Give us a few minutes, give us a few minutes, we'd say. And they hadn't the patience to wait that few minutes and they'd pull the cover off the top of the tent. And thank God it was lucky the Travellers never used to sleep without their clothes. The Travellers were modest and they wouldn't strip off their clothes in the tent. And I see you there, a pack of dogs all lyin' together, they'd say. But we wouldn't be. It was just maybe people would by lyin' together, children, mothers. But nothin' more than that went on. It was just the way mothers and their children lay together to keep themselves warm. And the police would stand and they'd laugh and jeer. And Jesus, the names that they used call us. Ye dirty Fenians. Go on ye pack o Fenians. You should be up and on to your own country. Yis not welcome down here. Who sent for yis down here? Women would be pleading mercy and at the same time they'd be calling them bad names back in the Cant under their tongue, all the names in the world. And the police'd say, What are you comin' out with your Irish for? They never used think it was the Cant. They used to think it was Irish. Calling us all the names and me mother'd be cursin' them back under her tongue.

Me father, God be good to him, he made everything. His whole business was makin' wagons. Wagons, tinware, jewellery, baskets, ornaments, traps, anything. Me father, God be good to him, he used to make everything. He made stuff for the settlers. He repaired stuff. He used to make stuff for me mother, jewellery and baskets, copper baskets that she could hawk out of. Almost everything he made. When me father died, we got rid of them then. D'you know the way Travellers get rid of everything when someone dies? So we had to get rid of our own wagon and everything with it because they didn't believe in keeping it. So that's the way it was.

There'd be a lot of sadness when someone'd die, and believe me there'd be no cookin'. Nobody'd cook. You know the way Travellers would be. They wouldn't be interested in food for those few days or say for a week.

Oh me father, now. Lord have mercy on him. I remember him now.
I remember him making the last wagon before he died. Me mother still talks about him a lot today. You had to have special wood for the lats of the wagon. You wouldn't get it everywhere. You had to have special lats and you'd have to wet them and you'd have to bind them. And a child wouldn't be allowed to go near them. You know you'd have the special material. And the four-wheeler would have to be sound and strong. They all had colours. The Irish wagons had all these colours and scrawls and painting. They had very strange scrawls and painting and flowers. They'd have a lovely fancy panbox in the back and that would hold the milk. It was all done in these fancy round designs and there'd be two lovely doors with little flowers or fruit or whatever, specially to match the wagon. It was the men, the men used to do it. Ah, I don't think they're as handy now. The men used to do it. You see, me father had nobody to leave that to because the boys were too young to learn when he died. So there was nobody to pick up the work from him, you know, they were only childer.

That's all gone now and it's a pity though. They don't keep it up today. When it came into the 60's – say 58, 59, 60 – the Travellers began to go into the cars or vans. That was their move, from the ponies and wagons to the cars and the trailers, that was their move.

March (continued)

Germany

President Herzog visits the Romani Holocaust Exhibition in Heidelberg.

Czech Republic

Four skinheads sentenced to prison, but for short terms, in connection with the death of Tibor Danihel (see 1993 above).

Romania

Conference in Bucharest on the Prevention of Violence and Discrimination against Roma in Europe.

April

Greece

Eviction of 100 Romani families from Ano Liosia. Partial resettlement in guarded camp.

June

Poland

Roma attacked in Wiebodzice.

Croatia

Seminar on Roma in Croatia today.

August

Czech Republic

Several hundred Roma fly to Canada to seek asylum.

You smug bastard

by Ian Hancock (England/U.S.)

Author's note: I wrote this 25 years ago after a harrowing
morning at the Canadian Embassy in London. I was trying to
emigrate to Canada to join my family there, but was refused
because my papers had "Romany" written on them. It took
more than a year and endless paperwork before I was allowed to
go. History repeated itself in 1997 when, at the invitation of the
Canadian government to come and speak on behalf of the
Czech Roma refugees, I was again detained and interrogated by
immigration officials for an hour, specifically because of the
nature of my visit, and despite my credentials, before being
allowed into the country.

You smug bastard
with your uniform and frozen smile.
How's *your* mother?
I haven't seen mine in quite a while.
A second opinion?
To hear again I'm not right
for your precious Canada?
"Not our type of immigrant"?
Too righteous for words.
No thanks.
We live our lives hearing this shit
from people like you.
Jailers, immigration officers, policemen.
No faces:
twelve million soundless throats
a thousand years of being pushed away
by *your* fathers and *your* children.
can you even begin to imagine
the feelings you've created?
I'm sorry. Let me try to be more like you.
Let me in. Let me embrace my father.
I won't be bad again.

November

Spain
European Congress of Romani Youth held in Barcelona.

Bulgaria
International conference on Romani children and their education.

Norway
Romani people are awarded the Rafto Human Rights Prize.

U.S.A
Second Rom member appointed by President Clinton to the U.S. Holocaust Memorial Council.

November/December

England
Romani refugees from the Slovak Republic arrive in Dover seeking asylum and receive mainly negative reactions and scepticism from local residents and the national news media.

In the recesses of the baroque wardrobes ...

by Attila Balogh (Hungary)

Message:
Dinner is in the fridge
Gran has died
I have taken the dog for a walk
Love Dad.

Do messages arranges themselves by right, need, ability, or does the message giver pre-select the subject matter according to his rights, needs, abilities or sometimes even dictatorship?

The dinner really is in the fridge

Gran really has died (note the Death Certificate and the tasteful engraving on the urn containing her ashes)

The dog, to our great annoyance, can indeed take itself for a walk in elegant parks amongst the trees which provide for its basic need while we gad about after it with our dodgy pacemakers.

Papa's kiss is only a traditional hypocrisy of a superior, of the bread winner and the bringer of today's news; it was as if Papa was the State.

The State, as a collected heap of family units, has, as a rule, a single cultural and economic origin. Therefore, standing to one side, by claiming our rights as individuals, produces those characteristics of a minority (at the social level) or of mental illness at the level of the individual.

It seems the world's newshounds have been struck dumb. Multinational companies form, overturning the economic character of ethnicity: English wool, Scottish whiskey, musical Hungarian Gypsies, Brussels's lace, Spanish flu, Russian vodka. Inter-ethnic environmental sexuality touches personal relationships: everyone can meet down at the global village disco.

Authorised by racism, the Ministry for Foreign Trade of Centraleurope Land exports its Gypsies to the Slave market in Dover, England, where they are disconnected from the respirator of their homeland. In the confusion of their coma, the Gypsies are made models of unpatriotism. Gentle English men and women, for your delight and delectation, we offer you Gypsies at the most competitive prices – no need to provide a receipt ...

In the aftermath of a few good conferences, the solidarity of the Play-Back button allows us to sing the songs of the slaves and of those who live on reservations, according to whom there is no God, there is no homeland. But there are plenty of scholars colonising the area of folklore research.

We simulate the abandonment of family ties when standing at the back of an elegant erotic disco, we let our eyes wander after a pretty piece of skirt. The forsaking of nation can also be ensured without the severity of a Mengele's science when, thanks to cloning, a large number of Gypsies can become acquainted with Norwegians.

Does it have any cultural-anthropological value, is it a cultural-anthropological activity if, despite my Gypsiness, I choose a Magyar woman? If we do not take account of love, the answer is yes.

Leaving aside the professional advice of geneticists and anthropologists, I avoided the girls from the slums and the young scientists keen to stuff a microphone into their mouths. My halting search for love and a home led me to the castle of a Hungarian aristocrat. At first there was panic but my winning personality and classical good looks meant that I could quickly overcome the divide between our two cultures. Thanks to my exotic physiognomy and my typically Aryan cranial development I was offered coffee and a bite to eat.

Greedily I took in the, for me, strange but nevertheless entertaining cultural items around me. I noticed, for instance, that to clean their bodies they used reduced froth bioactive soap. However, the cleansing of their corrupt spirits they leave to civil servants and tolerant judges. They don't pick their teeth in public and will only blow their nose into a monogrammed handkerchief with the head turned slightly to one side (in the way that Gypsies spit in the street). Children of different sexes and adults bathe separately in order to avoid too early a realisation of something essential. The sign of their civilisation is that they stare at a plastic box through ultra-violet eyeglasses and watch a never-ending story divided up into hundreds of episodes. Because of the structure of their early history, the problem of spiritual degeneration had been solved: the television smog that clings to their optic nerves obscures introspection.

There was once a king of Hungary who, as a result of diplomatic scheming, received his crown not from the Byzantium, but from the Holy Roman Empire. Thus Christianity came to Hungary as an alien, but necessary culture and administrative system. This king instructed his successors to welcome foreigners because a state with only one language and one culture would be destined to decline.

The poor king never knew that the Treaty of Trianon, which followed the end of World War One, would divide not only the settled and tolerated foreigners from their homeland, but also many Magyars as well as some Gypsies with their prosthetic identity as Hungarian speakers. Dear friends, the Magyars won every battle but failed to win a single war. Clearly, as a strategic model, this sends an important message to the Gypsy intelligentsia.

Our modern-day little kings are now obliged, before entering NATO or the European Union, to fall in love with the Gypsies for at least fifteen minutes and to demonstrate their enthusiasm for democracy before the various committees considering these applications. Therefore they created the National Gypsy Minority Self-Government to give apparent legitimacy to the Gypsies' constitutional rights. Well-organised apparatchiks carefully oversaw the fraud of electing Gypsy leaders, exploiting contradictions within the Gypsy intelligentsia to ensure the victory of easily programmed vassals. With foreign policy interests at stake, the Constitutional Court turned a blind eye to this electoral fraud. Everything is wonderful, everything is great, I am happy with it all, said the biggest of the little kings. Now the rebellious Gypsy intellectuals are lying low and, amidst the strains of authentic folk music, wait for a seat in Parliament, or a job in the Ministry.

On the other side of the global cerebrum, where tourists tread incognito, exists a new imperialism. The colonial power is the Hamburger Empire, its colony, the human spirit. Synthetic analysts fumble with the workings of the nervous system to explain the desire for and causes of rebellion and put them down as the onset of appendicitis. But the rupture can now only be cured by surgery. Beneath the stretched skin of the bubo, dormant puss conceals confrontation between many nationalities. The sick spirit must be taken to the ward specialising in ethnic operations where the infection of alien ethnicity can be professionally removed. Eventually, thanks to the autistic chants of monoglot surgeons, only a homogenous, mono-lingual, mon-cultural swelling remains.

Does the embrace or kiss of an "alien" cause ethnic problems? Is origin or individuality more dominant when stepping over the petrified and hierarchical threshold of excitement? Love is as much a result (if result at all) of relationships between individuals or between nations as the product of a mathematical equation containing two unknowns, between X and Y chromosomes.

A Hungarian poet with the talent of Shakespeare was once invited into the recesses of a centuries-old wardrobe of the baroque style where he was hidden away from the sight of his relatives. Beneath the creases of over-starched skirts he wrote "The Earth hangs in the void like an unripe lemon." What undigitalised bravery and passion did it take, without the aid of a laser slide-rule, to compare the Earth to an unripe lemon and, what's more, to describe it as hanging in a void! At that time the lemon was an unknown fruit in Hungary and the poet hardly more famous. What cause did they have to hide away the poet? Why secrete him from his cloth-capped or crown-bearing relatives who devour continents as if they were chewing gum? Both as a person and as a people, the poet became an orphan as soon as the doorbell rang.

The school-keepers of the world, the modern-day colonialists, raise the alarm against love and relationships between the nationalities in order to prove the superfluity of both. However, in the desert and in the recesses of the baroque wardrobes, the vitality of the human spirit awaits the redeeming monsoon rain.

Extracted from a paper given by Attila Balogh at Greenwich University, 1998; translated by Martin Kovats

1998

January

U.S.A

Last existing American law discriminating against Roma is rescinded in New Jersey.

Green, yellow, blue, red are the colours of my people

by Nadia Hava-Robbins (Czechoslovakia/U.S.A)

Green are the pastures, meadows and vast forest,
stems of flowers and shimmering leaves
on the proud brave trees reaching to the sun
surviving the gusty winds, lightning and storms.
Green is my bed and cool shadow
on a hot summer's day
soft grass where I lay my head.
Green is the taste of apples and pears
and the aroma of spring.
Green is where birds sing
and where I was born
and will be buried.

> Yellow are the sun's threads
> embroidering the tapestry of the land
> and wild dandelions like golden nuggets
> scattered along the roadside
> where children run and eagerly collect them
> as precious treasure.
> Yellow is the full moon casting light
> on the dark mystical velvet nights of dreams.

Blue
Blue is my soul
when I hear your song crying
the divine depth
the sky reflecting in waters of lakes and ponds
where speechless swimmers
are caught with bare hands for food
the free clean streams
satisfying our thirst for life, for freedom.
Blue are my veins
and through them a red river flows:
blood, what links us together.

    Red spins in my head
    hills of grapes and wine cellars
    and sweet barrels
    and vapours of deep red drunken melancholy.
    Red is the heat, the warmth of crackling fire
    the smell of food cooking
    the burning light
    the bright red sparkles among grey ashes
    and the eternal flames
    of desire, passion, devotion and love.
    Green, Yellow, Blue and Red:
    These are the colours of my people.

We did not break our century-old drums

by Alija Krasnići (Kosovo)

We did not break our
century-old drums
nor forsake our dancers
and players, half-dead
from cold; from those
who transformed our
voices and songs into
the ominous sound of
wounded nightbirds,
our secrets are hidden
in the legends and ashes
of our vanishing hearths.

We awaited the day
a silver-tipped bird
would fly over the ghetto;

our old people dreamed
of pristine white sails
afloat on the Pengebe river.

But the treacherous riders
of heaven-sent angels
took down the stars
from our crumbling houses;
our anguished eyes
saw a dark woman in
a torn dress, her
children in rags. Then
as the dust rose from
our unshod feet,
there appeared in
the mind a people,

hungry and homeless,
old, weary travellers:
they who have buried
their innermost hopes.
In the pores of a women,
living and breathing,
lies the burden of sorrows
endured by her ancestors
as they march down centuries
along the turbulent river.

In her lies the place
where reality meets
with a new beginning,
down a dirt road
towards a horizon
that ever recedes.

Without house or grave

by Rajko Djurić (Yugoslav Republic/Germany)

O-o-o
goes my endless lament

o-o-o
to my father-o
my graveless father
my homeless people
toys of the wind
dregs of the world

Where then
Where then from here?

o-o-o
to my mother-o
gentle mother
where is there a stone
on which to raise me up
that I might call your name?
The sky is our cover
and wherever I fly
the ground is barren
without a heart.

Where then
Where then from here?

... a life of wandering
forwards, backwards
along the roads
that time forgot.

Translated from French by Siobhan Dowd

Two Romani versions of *Without house or grave* are given here. The first is written in the original alphabet used by the author whilst the second is in the alphabet accepted by the Fourth International Romani Congress in Warsaw, April 1990.

Bi kheresqo bi limoresqo

Rajko Djurić (Yugoslav Republic/Germany)

O-o-o
lele mange sajek

o-o-o
joj dade morejana
Tu bi limoresko
Amen bi kheresko
Te avas e balvalake po phurdipe
e themeske po khandipe

Kaj maj
Džikaj maj

o-o-o
joj daje guglijena
Pe savo barh te ačhav
Katar tut te akharav
Phanglo si amenge o del
E phuv sargo kaj čuči si
bi khanikasko

Kaj maj
Džikaj maj

Kon pašavol
kon duravol
Maškar e xasarde droma trajimaske.

Bi kheresqo bi limoresqo

Rajko Djurić (Yugoslav Republic/Germany)

O-o-o
lele manqe savaxt

o-o-o
joj dad!e morre!ana
Tu bi limoresqo
Amen bi kheresqo
Te avas e balvalaqe p-o phudipe
e themesqe p-o khandipe

Kaj maj
ʒikaj maj

o-o-o
joj daj!e gugli!ene
Pe savo bar te aćhav
Katar tut te akharav
Phanglo si amenqe o del
E phuv sargo kaj ćući si
bi khanikasqe

Kaj maj
ʒikaj maj

Kon paśavol
kon duravol
Maśkar e xasarde droma ʒivdimasqe.

Biographies

Rajko Djurić

was born in Malo Orasje, near Belgrade, in 1947. After receiving a Diploma in Philosophy at the Philosophical Faculty in Belgrade, he went on to obtain a Doctorate of Sociology in 1986. As a Rom himself, he concentrates his writings – including his doctorate – mainly on the culture and history of the Romani. His poetry collection *Without House or Grave*, from which two of the poems here were taken, brings together the multifaceted history, ethnography, language, culture and politics of the Roma people. His aim is to portray how, despite the absence of any statehood or territory that the Roma people can call their own, they have managed to preserve their cultural identity. His literary works have been translated into more than five languages. He is the president of the International Romani Union and General Secretary of the Romani Centre of International PEN. He is presently living in exile in Berlin, Germany, having fled Yugoslavia to avoid conscription into the army during the Balkan war.

Siobhan Dowd

who conceived and oversaw this project, was for six years the Program Director of PEN American Center's Freedom-to-Write Committee in New York City where she established PEN's Threatened Literatures series. She is editor of another anthology, *This Prison Where I Live* (Cassell, 1996), and the author of more than a hundred articles – book reviews, essays, travel pieces – many of them addressing the subjects of human rights, censorship, and social repression. She lives in London and New York.

Ian Hancock

was born in Britain of both British and Hungarian Romani descent and has been active in the Romani movement since the 1960s. Currently Professor of Romani Studies at The University of Texas at Austin, he represents the Gypsy people at the United Nations and in UNICEF, and is the sole Romani member of the U.S. Holocaust Memorial Council. He was awarded the prestigious Rafto Human Rights Prize (Norway) for 1997, and was the 1998 recipient of the Gamaliel Chair in Peace and Justice. His publications on Roma number over 150, and include *The Pariah Syndrome: An Account of Gypsy Persecution and Slavery* (Karoma: Ann Arbor, 1987), and *A Handbook of Vlax Romani* (Slavica: Columbus, 1995).

Donald Kenrick

was born in London on the 6 June 1929, the descendant of Jewish Polish immigrants who left Poland around 1900 at the time of anti-semetic pogroms. He took a first–class honours degree in Arabic from London University, followed by a Master's on the image of the Jew in Scandinavian literature, for which he was required to master all the nordic languages as well as Hebrew and Yiddish. An enthusiast for the rights of small language groups, he was at one time contributor to a Cornish revivalist magazine. An enthusiasm for Bulgarian folkdance led him to a job teaching in Bulgaria, where he came into contact with the Romani language, eventually completing a PhD on the Drindari dialect. He co–authored, along with Gratton Puxon, the first full–length study of the Romani Holocaust, *The Destiny of Europes Gypsies* (Heinemann, 1972) and has served as secretary of the early Gypsy Council. He also worked voluntarily for the National Gypsy Education Council, and the Romani Guild. He is the author of *Gypsies: from India to the Mediterranean* (CRDP, 1993), *On the verge: the Gypsies of England.* 2nd edition (University of Hertfordshire Press, 1993), *Gypsies Under the Swastika* (University of Hertfordshire Press, 1995) and most recently *The Historical Dictionary of the Gypsies* (Scarecrow Press, 1998).

Gjünler Abdula

originally from Skopje, Macedonia, today lives in Holland. The poem featured here comes from his collection *Bizoagor/Eindeloos* (*Without End*) published in 1995. Abdula was born in 1965 and went to a technical high school. He worked as a reporter on a show about Romani issues called "Bird" broadcast on radio and TV in Macedonia. He has also worked as a theatre director for Romani students and for three years running – 1988, 1989, 1990 – he won a prize for the best amateur productions in the province. He was founder of a political party in the region representing Romani rights named "PSERM" and became the first Rom to be a member of the City Parliament in Skopje. He was also a member of a commission charged with looking into problems arising on religious grounds between Muslims and Christians. With the outbreak of war in the Balkans, however, and heightened ethnic tensions, he and his family began to receive death threats. In 1992, he decided to go into exile, first in Germany, then in Holland. He has been writing poems and plays since the age of 12 and has also translated numerous classic texts from Macedonian into Romani, including Shakespeare, Brecht, and Lorca.

Attila Balogh

is a poet and essayist of Romani origin writing in Hungarian. He was born in 1956 in the town of Sikso, north-eastern Hungary. Three books of his verses have been published in Hungary. Attila was a founding member of the Roma organisation "Phralipe" and edits the journal *Cigányfúró*. He is also director of the "Danube to the Ganges Foundation."

Dezider Banga

was born to a smith's family in 1939 near Lucenec in the Slovak Republic. He studied the Slovak language and history and went on to study philosophy at the University of Bratislava. He worked first as a grammar school teacher in Trebisov. Later he became a television producer in Košice. He writes in both Slovak and Romani. His first collection poems – *Piesen nad Vetrom* (*Songs above the Wind*) – was published in Slovak in 1964. Other publications followed: *Marsh Marigold and Water Lily* (poems, 1967), *Dialogues with Night* (poems, 1970), *Black Hair* (stories, 1970), *Blue Storm* (poems, 1970), *Burning Cherry* (poems, 1982), and *The Fading Magnolias* (poems, 1989). All of these publications address Gypsy themes. He has also written many plays, some for television. In 1969, he founded the society Romani Kultura. A collector of Romani songs, he lives today in Bratislava and is chief editor of the periodical *Roma*.

Béla Osztojkán

was born in 1948 in Cserger, Hungary. He graduated from secondary school in 1971 and worked as an unskilled physical worker and a printing house proofreader. He lives some of the time in Budapest, Hungary, where, as well as being a poet he runs "Phralipe", a social/political Romani organisation dedicated to promoting the rights of the Roma living in Hungary. The rest of his time he spends in Debrecen, also in Hungary. He is married, with children, to a Hungarian social worker who runs and inner-city education centre for Romani youth. His first book of poems was published in 1981. His titles to date include *Fish in a Black Zither* (poetry, 1981); *Snowfall in Faithfulness* (poetry, 1983); *God isn't Home* (short stories, 1985); and *Nobody will pay for Atyin Joska* (a novel, 1997). He is described by his friends as a "mild-mannered poet-philosopher."

Luminiţa Mihai Cioabă

was born in 1957 in Romania. A journalist and poet, she won first prize for poetry in the 2nd Amici Rom contest. Her poetry includes two collections published in Romani, Romanian, German and English under the titles *The Roots of the Earth* and *The Rain Merchant*. She has also written two plays. Between 1991 and 1994, she was editor-in-chief of the periodical *Neo Drom*. She has also authored *Under a Sky's Corner*, a collection of fairy tales inspired by Romani traditions. She writes in both Romani and Romanian, but she says that she prefers to write in Romani when possible as she finds that "its syntax and treasure of words is richer and best suits my needs." "But I find writing in Romanian convenient, too," she adds, "as I truly believe that I could contribute – modestly perhaps – to drawing together and enriching reciprocally these two languages that my people and family were born and formed in." On the subject of why she writes, she says, "The Roma people represent one of the most ancient cultures in history and I find it extremely exciting to know that they can now fully express themselves and to make known their rich sensibility. I am proud to have a part in this rebirth and claim my right to say my word too."

Nadia Hava-Robbins

was born in Prague in the former Czechoslovakia. She spent most of the year in the city with her parents, disguising, as she says, her Romani origins: "As kids, we were specifically instructed to remain silent regarding our ethnic heritage, and that is no wonder, since our parents and grandparents only barely escaped the persecution of World War II." She spent the summers in the countryside of southern Slovakia with her grandparents and here her extended family used to gather and observe the Romani traditions of music, dance, stories and family customs. When she was 15, she emigrated to the USA Some twenty years later, she began writing poetry: "My soul awakened with a creative spark, and I began to explore my people's origin, write poetry, and dance in the name of my ancestry." Several of her poems have been published in both English and Romani and have appeared in the National Library of Poetry anthologies under the titles *The Space Between, Echoes of Yesterday*, and *Best Poems of 1995*.

Hester Hedges

was born in 1980 and was 16 when she wrote the poem *A Wooden Rose*. She now lives near Cambridge and is studying Modern History, English Language and Sociology at a sixth form college. She is the daughter of two Gypsies who have been settled for the last 12 years – "We were lucky enough to get a license for our trailer – perhaps about 90 per cent of our people are not so lucky." She plans to study law at University in September 1998. "I don't have this huge thing inside me to write about oppression since I think that most Travellers don't worry about what other people think about them. But since I've been four I have seen Travellers come and go. Because I've been in one place I've seen everything moving around me. I am writing if you like because there are things I wanted to say to them before they moved on. I am writing from a middle point of view".

José Heredia Maya

was born in 1947 in Albunelas in Granada Province, Spain. He is a poet, playwright and essayist and one of the best known Gypsies writing in Spanish. An expert on the works of Frederico Garcia Lorca, he is a doctor in Spanish literature and a Professor of Spanish Philology at the University of Granada. Among his best known works are the collections of poems: *Penar Ocono* (1973), *Charrol* (1983), *Un Gitano de Ley* (1997). He is also the author of the three plays *Camelamos Nakerar* (1976), *Macama Jonda* (1983) and *Sueno Terral* (1990).

Bairam Haliti

is a Rom living in Gnjilalic in the former Yugoslavia. His poems have appeared in the anthology, edited by Alexian Santino Spinello, published each year to represent the best submissions to the international "Amico Rom" competition. At time of press, no further information was available.

Šaban Iliaz

a poet from Šuto Orizari in Macedonia, began writing poems at an early age and by 20 was a published poet. His poems have been broadcast over Radio Skopje. He is a member of the cultural group Phralipe (Brotherhood) and has participated in many Roma festivals in Europe.

Sandra Jayat

was born in 1938 near the border of France and Italy. As a young girl, she travelled with her Manouche family and was living near Lake Maggiore in Italy when she decided against an arranged marriage. She made her way alone to Paris where she met Django Reinhardt, a cousin of hers, before he died in 1953. Self-educated, she found work as a commercial artist and has exhibited her work in the Grand Palais Salon, and the Musée Bourdelle. In 1992, the French Government commissioned her to create a postage stamp depicting "travelling people". Her first book of poems was published in 1961. A self-styled "daughter of the wind" her themes are closeness to nature, guitar music, true friendship and the freedom of the road. The poem *Django* printed here appeared first in *Nomad Moons* (Brentham Press, 1995).

Nicolas Jimenes Gonzalez

was born in Spain in 1968. He has lived in Argentina and Poland, but now resides in his native Madrid, where he works as a sociologist and Romani activist. He writes stories and poems, and some of the latter have appeared in anthologies such as the Amico Rom award run by Alexian Santino Spinelli (see below). He speaks both Romani and Spanish, but writes in Spanish as he says he "knows it better." He often chooses to spell Spanish words in the way the Roma in Spain spell them as a way of stamping his identity on his work. "When I introduce some of these words or structures," he reports, "I feel my work is warmed and more immediate than if I had used the Academy's Spanish." He began writing as a teenager in an effort to convey his "personal version of the surrounding reality." Today he writes as "a witness for the defence of my people and our culture." In his work as a sociologist, he has encountered racism regularly and has seen his fellow Roma suffering from violence inflicted on them because of their ethnicity.

Valdemar Kalinin

was born in 1946 in Vitebsk, Belarus, but now lives in London. His poetry has appeared in *Rrom p-o Drom*, Roma on the Road, (published in Poland) and *Linguistica* (published in the Czech Republic). He speaks both Romani and Belarussian, but states categorically that he prefers to write in Romani, in stanzas that rhyme and scan. In his country, he reports that his people face racism continually and his strong desire to write comes partly from his aspiration to "understand the role of the oneness of all Roma." He believes that this will be impossible without having literature published in the Romani language.

Alija Krasnići

was born in 1952 at Obilić in Kosovo. He is author of *Ĉergarendje jaga* (*The fires of the tent-dwelling Gypsies*), the first ever book of tales in Romani to be published in the Yugoslav Republic. All the stories in this collection are pessimistic in outlook, save the last, "Mihrija", which is about a woman who leads her family to a better life. He has also written two plays, *Romano ratvalo abav* (*Romani Blood Wedding*) and *Tsara me, tsara tu* (*A little bit me, a little bit you*) which have been performed by a Romani theatre group in Obilić, Kosovo, where Krasnici now lives with his family. The poem "We did not break our century old drums" was first published in the anthology *Amico Rom*, edited by Alexian Santino Spinello and published annually to represent the best submissions to the international Amico Rom competition.

Gregory Dufunia Kwiek

was born in 1968 to Romani parents who were from Russia but had moved to Poland. When the communists came to power in Poland his family moved away and dispersed around the world. Kwiek has travelled the world. "Many non-Gypsies believe I have led a glamorous life," recounts Kwiek, "because of my travelling. Yes, I have enjoyed some of it, but the reasons for my travel were not so enjoyable. I was driven into a life of constant running because of the fears and mistrust of Non-Gypsy and because of my own fears of them. My travels are not those of freedom, as so many think." His travels meant he was only educated to the age of about 12 and he often felt forced to conceal his identity as a Rom to ensure that he got work. He has worked in many trades. On reading Dr. Ian Hancock's book *The Pariah Syndrome* Kwiek reports that he underwent a radical change. "I understood the history behind my problems and realized it was time to live my life as I was, a Rom. Being equipped with this knowledge I am now able to fight both my fears and the fears of the non-Gypsies as well." Kwiek now runs his own company Romani Movement Entertainment from Staten Island, New York.

Andro Loleshtye

is thought to be a poet from the former Soviet Union. The poem "Ars Poetica" appeared in both a Romani and English version in the influential journal *Roma* edited by Leksa Manuš. At time of press, no further information about the poet was available.

Djura Makhotin

was born in 1951 in Azerbaijan, but now lives in Tver in Russia. He is both a journalist and musician and runs a Romani club called Romengro Lav (Romani World) which regularly broadcasts programs in Romani on the local station. He also defends local Roma who have been harassed by the police. In his literary work, he has experimented with combining the northern and southern dialects of Russian Romani and has published a grammar on the subject called *Handbook for the Romani Language*. He is currently working on a story based on the life of Jesus Christ and has also translated many parts of the Bible. His poetry has appeared in the journal *Rrom p-o Drom* (Roma on the Road) and elsewhere and he directs a local music ensemble that has won many awards at international festivals.

Leksa Manuš

to whose memory this book is dedicated, was born Aleksandr Aledzunz-Belugins at Riga, Latvia, in 1942 and died in 1997. He was a world-renowned Rom, a linguist, writer and poet. For several years he worked as a research librarian at Moscow's Institute of Scientific Information, a centre which prepares two bulletins, one on foreign literature, the other on (the then) 'Soviet' literature. Following his long military service in Kazakhstan, he wrote a story *Where are you, Roma?* He mastered many Romani dialects and one of his major accomplishments was the translation into Romani of the Indian classic *The Ramayana*. He was a prominent contributor to the Journal *Roma* over many years and did much to encourage new, younger, Romani writers, especially poets, to come to the fore. He was also the editor of an anthology of Gypsy poetry and author of a Romani ABC for Russian and Latvian Roma.

Matéo Maximoff

was born in Barcelona in 1917. His mother was a tightrope walker at a circus, his father a Gypsy from Southern Russia. The Maximoffs were part of the Belkeshti clan. An orphan at 14, Maximoff had to earn a living for himself and his siblings as a movie projectionist. In 1938 he was sent to prison because of his involvement in a fight between two clans. While in prison Maximoff wrote his first novel *The Ursitory*. The book was only published after World War II in 1946 because during the Nazi occupation Maximoff was interned in a concentration camp in the Pyrenees. *The Price of Liberty*, about the revolt of Romani slaves in Romania, was published in 1955. He has published six novels as well as numerous short stories, essays and poetry, and has also translated the Bible into the Romani language. His literary style is akin to the Magic Realism of Latin America in that it incorporates the magic of myth and folklore into realistic narratives. Maximoff continues to live and work in Romainville near Paris. He writes in both Romani and French, and says that he sees it as his task to make known the truth about the Roma without embellishment.

Mariella Mehr

was born in Zürich in 1947 as the child of Jenische parents. The Jenische are a travelling people in Switzerland and not believed to be related to the Roma, although there are many cultural similarities. Mehr's autobiographical first novel *Stone Age* (*Steinzeit*, 1981) depicts her difficult childhood, much of which she spent in reform schools and psychiatric institutions as a victim of the Swiss government's "socialization" program. The book was highly acclaimed, and she has published poetry, three more novels, an essay collection as well as a play following this success. Mariella Mehr lives in Bern and on the road.

Papusza

is regarded by Romani writers today as the mother of Romani poetry. "Papusza", meaning "doll", was her Romani name; her official name was Bronislawa Wajs. She was born c. 1910 to a Romani family in Poland and married a harpist named Dionizy Wajs who interested her in Romani song. During World War Two, she survived the Nazi occupation of Poland by hiding in the forests – an experience which permeates much of her later work, including the extract published in this volume. In 1949, the Polish poet Gerzy Ficowski met Papusza, collected her poems and brought them to public attention. Unfortunately, since he backed the government's declared plan to settle all nomads, Papusza's asociation with him caused her to be seen by her own people as a collaborator with this policy. She was expelled from her clan in 1956 and lived the rest of her life in isolation. She died in 1987.

Margita Reiznerová

was born in 1945 in Maly Bukovec, Eastern Slovakia, to a family of Romani blacksmiths. Her sisters Helena and Milena and her brothers Arnost and Lada also write short stories, tales, and legends. Immediately after the war the family migrated to Prague, as the part of Slovakia where they lived had been destroyed. In Prague Margita worked in a hospital as an auxilliary nurse until poor health forced her to retire. She was active as a singer in a folk group led by her brother Lada known as "Perumos". In 1990 Margita was elected as a chair of the Association of Romani writers in what was then Czechoslovakia. She has published six books of Romani prose as well as her poetry and has translated the works of Chekhov into Romani. Her most recent publication is *Kali*, a collection of stories about the goddess. In Autumn 1996 the whole extended family emigrated to Belgium from fear of skin-head attacks.

Paola Schöpf

also called Kiriassa (Cherry), was born in Bolzano on the 23 February 1953. At the age of eleven, as a result of a family tragedy, she was given shelter as a boarder at a college in Verona where the intention was that she would study to become a teacher. Before she completed her examinations, however, she abandoned everything to return to her family in the South Tyrol in Northern Italy. She belongs to the musically talented Sinti Estrekharja from Austria. Her poems, written in Italian, have appeared in the anthology, edited by Alexian Santino Spinello, published each year to represent the best submissions to the international "Amico Rom" competition.

Charlie Smith

is a Gypsy poet living in a mobile home in Essex, England. Aged 42, he is the author of several titles including *Gavvered All Arond*, *Spirit of Flame*, *Not all Wagons and Lanes* and *No Savage Camping* (forthcoming). He normally writes in English, but uses Romani words "when it feels appropriate to do so." He is also a local Labour Party Councillor. He reports a long history or repression as a result of his ethnic origin. He remembers insults from teachers and pupils at school and for many years, the local Tory Party councillor (whom he defeated in the last election) tried to evict him from his home. One of the worst occasions was a Christmas Eve, when local police kicked in the door of his caravan on the pretext of inspecting a dog licence. He wife was nine months pregnant at the time. Smith writes, on the occasion of the publication of this anthology, that the most important challenge for the Roma today is to "make sure our children are educated and fully aware of our people's history and to take our rightful place as equal citizens of Europe with equal rights and respect for our culture."

Alexian Santino Spinelli

is a Rom, born in 1964 in the Abruzzi region of Italy. The youngest of six, he lives in Lanciano where he is married with three children and director of a music school. Spinelli describes himself as a "singer, songwriter, teacher, poet, and essayist." He is just about to graduate from the University of Bologna with a degree in foreign languages and literature. A frequent guest on television and radio shows, he is the founder and leader of a musical ensemble called the "Alexian Group" which regularly performs Gypsy music in Italy and abroad. He has recorded four albums and one CD. He has also received national awards for his literary works. His international contest of Romani art and literature called "Amico Rom" (Friend Rom) has led to five published anthologies of the submitted works and has contributed greatly to the current flowering of new Romani literature. His theatrical works written in Romani have been performed in Italy and France. Finally, Spinelli is president of the cultural association "Them Romano" ("Romani World"), as well as director of the trimestral journal of the same name.

Jimmy Storey

lives in Australia. He was born in the United Kingdom and has lived in Papua New Guinea. As well as many articles and poems published in various journals, he has published a volume of poems under the title *Over There* (Far Possum Press, New South Wales, 1983). He writes in English and is currently learning Romani. His aim as a writer is to demonstrate to "gajé" readers the diversity of the real Roma world and to help empower Romani readers to "get beyond the limitations pre-supposed by identity within one group." He believes the main challenges facing the Roma today is – "getting enough to eat," then getting the freedom to choose "whether to live in a house or on the road ... Added to this, freedom from attack, injury, or death by the trained rottweilers of the new fascists."

Chrissie Ward

was born in 1947 in the Republic of Ireland. She sites her place of residence as "nowhere and everywhere". She has written poems which she says she has never tried to publish herself, but some have appeared in specialist publications about Ireland's Travellers or been used in schools. She reports that she and her family have suffered racist attacks all through their lives and she writes to take the troubles from her mind. "I have never thought of being a writer," she says, "I just wrote my thoughts down to leave to my family and for the sake of history. If racism ever stops, they won't believe what happened and the way it was in the past. It's important to remind them where their roots come from." She adds that the most important task for all Travellers is to win freedom and the right to write, to choose their own way of life and fight all discrimination.

Sterna Weltz-Zigler

was born in Avignon and grew up in Saintes-Maries-de-la-Mer in the Camargue region of France, living in a caravan. As a young woman, she made a living by making dolls of wickerwork which she sold in the market places. She moved to Paris and found a second home in Montmartre, the one place where she felt she could be at once settled and free. She has been writing poems since the age of 14 and has never lost the need to write. Her publications include the collection *Romanes*, from which the poem featured here is taken, and a memoir entitled *My Gypsy Secrets*. She is also founder of a music group called Rumberos where she recites her poems, accompanied by four Gypsy guitarists. Today, she lives partly in Paris and partly on the road and is married to Torino Zigler, a Romani painter, with whom she has collaborated on many projects.

Specially commissioned translators

Burton Bollag

orginally from New York, has been living in Prague since 1990 but is about to move to Bratislava. He covers Europe for *The Chronicle of Higher Education*, an American newspaper and is a former reporter for *The New York Times*.

Julie Elbin

is a young American writer and poet living in Princetown, Rhode Island. She graduated from Brown University two years ago.

Tom Fugalli

is a copywriter and freelance editor living in New York. His poetry has appeared in various literary magazines.

Martin Kovats

is a political scientist and in 1998 he completed his doctoral thesis on the development of Roma politics in Hungary.

Ruth Partington

has photographed Gypsies and written about Romani issues for several years. She has already translated Sandra Jayat's poems and is now working on her works of prose. She is a poet in her own right, her works having appeared in various literary magazines. She lives in St Albans.

Minna Proctor

is a writer and translator living in Brooklyn, New York and Tuscany. She is presently working on a translation of the short stories of Italian Modernist writer Federigo Tozzi as well as a collection of her own short stories.

Sinéad ní Shuinéar

a cultural anthropologist, has a thirty-year history of working on Irish Traveller issues and writing on ethnic issues generally. A graduate of Jagiellonian University in Krakow, Poland, she is also a translator from Polish, Italian and French.

Anika Weiss

will soon finish her MFA degree in fiction at Columbia University, New York. She is working on her first novel and freelances as a German/English translator. She lives in New York City.

Ian MacAndless

is Professor of English Literature at the University of Granada in Spain.